Speak Your Dream: Learn the 7Ms Canvas for Buzz-Worthy Speeches

By G.A. Johnson

KMeanz, Inc. dba AudAngle

1079 W Round Grove Rd

Lewisville, TX 75057

Copyright © 2023 by G.A. Johnson

All rights reserved.

ISBN: 978-0-9789436-7-7

Printed in USA/TX

© 2023 by G. A Johnson

All rights reserved. No part of this book may be reproduced in any form without permission in writing from the author, except by a reviewer who may quote brief passages in a review to be printed in a magazine, newspaper, or on the web.

Cover design by KMeanz, Inc.

ISBN: 978-0-9789436-7-7

Printed in the United States of America

Publisher information:

KMeanz, Inc.

www.audangle.com

First Edition: August 2023

Library of Congress Cataloging-in-Publication Data:

Johnson, G. A.

Speak Your Dream: Learn the 7Ms Canvas for Buzz-Worthy Speeches

ISBN: 978-0-9789436-7-7

Dedicated to Rustites.

By their fruits ye shall know them.

A Symphony of Speech: The 7 Ms

In the kingdom of speeches, under rhetoric's tree, Lay seven mighty M's, as wise as can be, Each one a character, a voice in the chorus, Together they sing; let's explore them before us.

Messenger, the hero, strong and bold, With authenticity, their story's told, Whether a prince or a jester, in their own right, They speak with passion, deep into the night.

Message, the heart, where the magic's found, It beats with purpose, a resonant sound, A treasure of ideas, arguments, and thoughts, Without it, dear friends, we're simply distraught!

Medium, the vessel, sleek and refined, Carries the words through space and time, A parchment, a stage, a digital screen, It's where the Message and Members convene.

Members, the crowd, with ears all aglow, From young to old, they gather to know, The secrets, the tales, the wisdom you share, They listen, they learn, and they truly care.

Monitoring, the scout, with a keen eagle's eye, Watches and learns from the distant sky, The impact, the changes, the shifts in the breeze, A speech's effect on hearts and minds, if you please!

Mobilization, the knight, with a call to arms, Inspires action with charismatic charms, A quest, a mission, a purpose so grand, He leads the Members to a promised land.

Moment, the finale, where all unite, A crescendo of voices in the moonlit night, A time and a place where magic's revealed, The speech is complete, and the deal is sealed.

So here's to the M's, in their glorious band, Guiding speakers and dreamers across the land, May your words be merry, and your voices ring true, For the 7 Ms are always here, cheering for you!

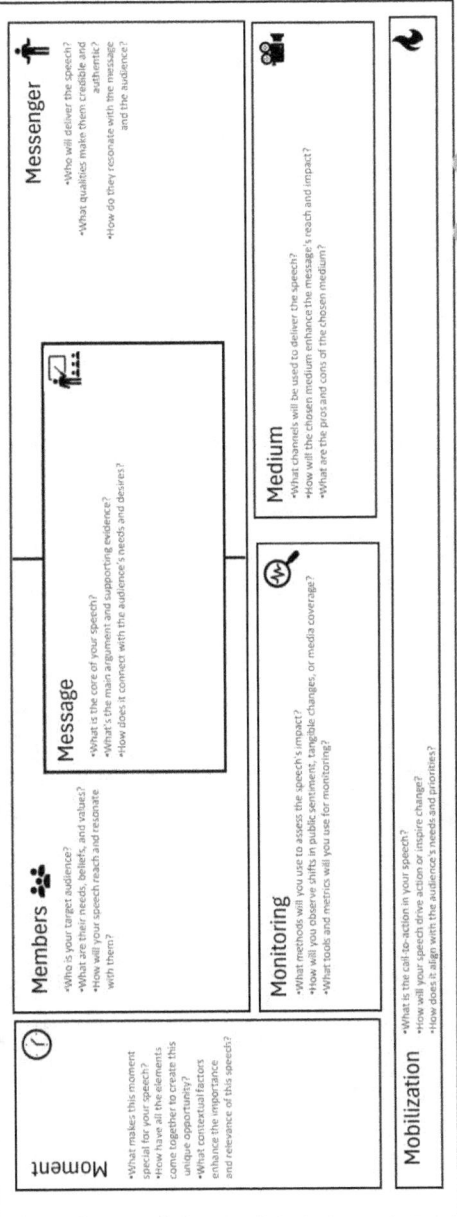

Table of Contents

Introduction		1
Chapter 1	The Members	4
Chapter 2:	The Messenger	32
Chapter 3:	The Message	60
Chapter 4:	The Moment	74
Chapter 5:	Monitoring	102
Chapter 6:	The Medium	132
Chapter 7:	Mobilization	168
Conclusion		
Appendix	7Ms The Speaker's Canvas	183

Introduction

The 7 Ms: The Public Speaker's Canvas is a powerful tool designed to guide speakers through the multifaceted process of crafting and delivering impactful speeches. A speech is a project, a construction of ideas, emotions, and actions, carefully arranged to resonate with its audience. From the initial preparation to the final moment of delivery, these seven key elements come together to create a symphony of communication. Embrace the journey of speechmaking, for your voice has the power to change the world, one word at a time.

Mastery of Prep

Embrace preparation as your cornerstone. The Mastery of Prep involves deep research and understanding of your audience, crafting your message, selecting the right messenger and medium, planning your mobilization strategy, and setting up monitoring systems. It is the blueprint that lays the foundation for all that follows.

Messenger

The Messenger is the voice of your speech. It's about choosing the right person to deliver your message, someone with the credibility and authenticity to connect with the audience. The Messenger's personality, ethos, and tone align with the core message, enhancing its impact.

Message

At the heart of the canvas lies the Message. It is the essence, the core argument, and the supporting evidence that binds everything together. It's where the meeting of minds between the Messenger and the Members takes place, resonating with truth, conviction, and purpose.

Medium

The Medium is the channel through which your speech flows. It can be a live presentation, a recorded video, written text, or other forms of communication. The Medium shapes the sensory experience of the audience, conveying the Message in a way that resonates with their hearts and minds.

Members

Members are the audience, the people you wish to reach and inspire. Understanding who they are, their needs, beliefs, and values, is key to crafting a Message that speaks to them directly. Reach them where they are and lead them to where they need to be.

Monitoring

Monitoring is the reflective lens through which you observe the impact of your speech. It includes assessing shifts in public sentiment, tangible changes, media coverage, and more. It's about fine-tuning the outcome and learning for the future, understanding that you can control the preparation and delivery but must adapt to the response.

Mobilization

Mobilization drives action. It is the call-to-action, the alignment of your Message with the audience's needs and priorities. How will your speech inspire change, motivate decisions, or provoke thought? Mobilization creates a bridge between words and deeds.

Moment

The Moment is the culmination, the time and place where everything comes together. It's the recognition of the unique circumstances that make this particular speech special, significant, and timely. It's the realization that all the Ms have worked in harmony to create an unforgettable experience.

By understanding and implementing these 7 Ms in your speechmaking journey, you'll find a new way to view the process, akin to an entrepreneur using a business model canvas. Whether you're a young leader or a seasoned professional, the 7 Ms and this canvas are your guides to speechmaking excellence.

Chapter 1: Members

Introduction: The Importance of Understanding Members (Audience)

1) Why Understanding Members is Important
The heart of any speech lies in its audience - the members who are there to listen, learn, and hopefully engage. A speech can be beautifully crafted and delivered, but if it fails to resonate with the audience, it falls short of its potential. Therefore, understanding the audience, or the members, is a cornerstone in effective public speaking.

2) Historical and Recent Anecdote Why Understanding Members is Important

- **Historical Anecdote**: In 431 BCE, Pericles delivered his famous Funeral Oration to honor those who had died in the Peloponnesian War. Aware of his audience's grief and pride, he tailored his speech to their emotions, offering consolation and inspiring a sense of national identity. This deep connection with the members made his speech a timeless piece of rhetoric.

- **Recent Anecdote**: At the 2018 commencement ceremony at Harvard University, Oprah Winfrey spoke to graduates about the power of service. Knowing her audience of young, ambitious individuals ready to step into the world, she tailored her message to inspire them to use their education for a greater good. The connection with the audience's aspirations turned a ceremonial address into a motivational masterpiece.

3) Relating it to the Speaker's Canvas

Understanding members is not a solitary component of the Speaker's Canvas but permeates all other elements. From shaping the message to choosing the right medium and monitoring reactions, knowing the audience guides every step of speech preparation and delivery.

4) Details Discussing Key Advice or Considerations for Improving Understanding of Members

- **Know Your Audience**: Understanding demographics, interests, and needs helps in crafting a message that resonates.

- **Engage with the Members**: Asking questions, making eye contact, and being receptive to their responses builds a connection.

- **Adapt to Feedback**: Be ready to adjust your speech based on the audience's reactions.

5) Three More Anecdotes

- **Contemporary**: In a 2019 TED Talk, climate activist Greta Thunberg spoke directly to the concerns of her generation. By understanding her peer audience, she could speak authentically and powerfully.

- **Historical Figure**: Winston Churchill, in his wartime speeches, connected with the fears and hopes of the British public, turning phrases that still resonate today.
- **Historical Figure**: Martin Luther King Jr., through his profound understanding of the civil rights struggle, was able to communicate in a way that mobilized millions.

6) Practical Advice How the User Can Improve Their Speech Understanding Members

- **Survey the Audience**: Before the speech, gather information on who will be attending.

- **Be Present**: Engage with the audience before, during, and after the speech.

- **Analyze Feedback**: Reflect on audience reactions and learn for the future.

7) Conclusion

Understanding the members of an audience is the bedrock upon which successful public speaking is built. It's a continuous process of learning, adapting, and growing, vital to any speaker's success.

Emotional Intelligence & Connection: Connecting with Members

1) Why Emotional Intelligence and Connection with Members are Important

Emotional Intelligence (EI) is the ability to perceive, understand, and manage one's emotions and those of others. In the context of public speaking, EI is paramount for connecting with your audience or members. A speaker who can empathize, resonate, and connect with the feelings of the audience creates a more engaging and memorable speech experience.

2) Historical and Recent Anecdote Why Emotional Intelligence and Connection are Important

- **Historical Anecdote**: During the dark days of the Great Depression, President Franklin D. Roosevelt used his Fireside Chats to connect emotionally with the American people. His soothing tone and empathetic words helped to ease the fears of a troubled nation.

- **Recent Anecdote**: Brene Brown's TED Talk on vulnerability is a modern-day example of emotional intelligence in action. By openly sharing her personal struggles and emotions, she created an immediate connection with the audience, making her talk one of the most viewed of all time.

3) Relating it to the Speaker's Canvas

Within the framework of the 7 Ms speaker's canvas, emotional intelligence is interwoven through various stages, from understanding the audience's (members') emotions in the preparation phase to monitoring and responding to their reactions during the speech.

4) Details Discussing Key Advice or Considerations for Improving Emotional Intelligence and Connection

- **Empathize with Your Audience**: Put yourself in their shoes to understand their needs, concerns, and emotions.

- **Use Storytelling**: Stories can help evoke emotions and create a stronger bond with the members.

- **Reflect on Your Emotions**: Understand and manage your emotions to maintain control and authenticity in your speech.

5) Three More Anecdotes

- **Contemporary**: Malala Yousafzai, in her speeches, connects deeply with audiences through her genuine compassion and commitment to education, making her words resonate globally.

- **Historical Figure**: Mahatma Gandhi, through his simple and heartfelt words, was able to mobilize a nation. His understanding of the people's plight made him a charismatic speaker.

- **Historical Figure**: Nelson Mandela's inaugural speech in 1994 showcased his emotional intelligence as he spoke of reconciliation and healing, striking a chord with a divided nation.

6) Practical Advice How the User Can Improve Their Speech Connecting with Members

- **Build Emotional Awareness**: Recognize and understand both your emotions and those of the audience.
- **Engage Authentically**: Be genuine and sincere in your delivery.
- **Practice Active Listening**: Respond to audience reactions and questions with empathy and understanding.

7) Conclusion

Emotional intelligence is not just a buzzword but a vital skill in public speaking. Connecting with the members on an emotional level turns a speech from a mere presentation into a meaningful conversation. It's a human touch that transcends boundaries and leaves a lasting impact.

Anecdotes: Successful Engagement with Different Audiences

1) Why Successful Engagement with Different Audiences is Important

No two audiences are the same. The ability to engage various groups, from students to professionals, from local communities to global forums, is a hallmark of an effective speaker. Tailoring your approach and anecdotes to each unique audience ensures a more personal and impactful connection.

2) Historical and Recent Anecdote Why Successful Engagement with Different Audiences is Important

- **Historical Anecdote**: In her lifetime, Eleanor Roosevelt spoke to a wide variety of groups, from coal miners to world leaders. Her ability to relate to different audiences made her a beloved and influential speaker.
- **Recent Anecdote**: Simon Sinek's "Start with Why" has been delivered in various forms to corporate executives, educators, and entrepreneurs. He adjusts his examples and anecdotes to connect with each specific audience, making his message resonate widely.

3) Relating it to the Speaker's Canvas

Successful engagement with various audiences fits into the framework of understanding Members in the 7 Ms speaker's canvas. Knowing who you are speaking to guides every part of the speech process, from preparation to delivery.

4) Details Discussing Key Advice or Considerations for Engaging Different Audiences

- **Analyze Your Audience**: Understand their background, interests, and expectations.

- **Use Relevant Anecdotes**: Share stories that are relatable to that specific audience.

- **Adjust Your Tone and Language**: Different audiences may require varying levels of formality and jargon.

5) Three More Anecdotes

- **Contemporary**: Michelle Obama, in her book tours and talks, has showcased her ability to connect with diverse audiences, from young students to business leaders.
- **Historical Figure**: Mark Twain's speaking engagements ranged from literary salons to labor unions, and his ability to tailor his speeches made him a sought-after speaker.
- **Historical Figure**: Susan B. Anthony's tireless efforts in speaking to various groups, from politicians to ordinary citizens, helped advance the women's suffrage movement.

6) Practical Advice How the User Can Improve Their Speech Engaging Different Audiences

- **Do Your Research**: Understand the specific audience you'll be addressing.

- **Be Flexible**: Be prepared to adjust your delivery based on audience reactions.

- **Practice with Diversity**: If possible, rehearse your speech in front of varied groups to get diverse feedback.

7) Conclusion

A one-size-fits-all approach rarely works in public speaking. Understanding and engaging with different audiences requires a keen awareness, adaptability, and genuine desire to connect. It's this tailored approach that turns a good speaker into a great one, able to reach hearts and minds across diverse landscapes.

Cultural Sensitivity & Global Perspective: Tailoring to Different Cultures

1) Why Cultural Sensitivity and Global Perspective are Important

In our increasingly interconnected world, speakers often find themselves addressing audiences from diverse cultural backgrounds. Recognizing and respecting these cultural nuances is not just polite; it's crucial to effective communication. A lack of cultural sensitivity can lead to misunderstandings and alienation, while understanding and embracing cultural diversity can enhance connection and engagement.

2) Historical and Recent Anecdote Why Cultural Sensitivity and Global Perspective are Important

- **Historical Anecdote**: When President John F. Kennedy spoke in Berlin in 1963, he uttered the famous line, "Ich bin ein Berliner." His effort to connect with the German audience by speaking their language (though debated in interpretation) was a symbolic gesture of solidarity and understanding.
- **Recent Anecdote**: In her international talks on human rights, Amal Clooney tailors her speeches to respect and reflect the cultural norms and values of

different countries. Her global perspective allows her to engage with various cultures meaningfully.

3) Relating it to the Speaker's Canvas

The understanding of cultural differences falls under the concept of Members in the 7 Ms speaker's canvas. It goes beyond knowing the audience's age or profession and delves into their values, beliefs, and traditions.

4) Details Discussing Key Advice or Considerations for Improving Cultural Sensitivity

- **Educate Yourself**: Learn about the cultural norms and values of the audience you are addressing.

- **Use Inclusive Language**: Avoid stereotypes and use language that respects different perspectives.

- **Show Genuine Interest**: Ask questions and show curiosity about different cultural viewpoints.

5) Three More Anecdotes

- **Contemporary**: Malala Yousafzai's speeches on education resonate across cultures, as she carefully considers cultural contexts in her advocacy.

- **Historical Figure**: Swami Vivekananda's address at the 1893 Parliament of the World's Religions displayed an understanding of both Eastern and Western philosophies.

- **Historical Figure**: Nelson Mandela, in promoting peace and reconciliation, always considered South Africa's rich cultural tapestry.

6) Practical Advice How the User Can Improve Their Speech Tailoring to Different Cultures

- **Seek Guidance**: If unsure, consult with someone familiar with the specific culture.
- **Avoid Assumptions**: Don't assume familiarity with certain concepts or idioms that may not translate well.
- **Embrace Diversity**: Recognize that cultural diversity enriches the conversation.

7) Conclusion

Cultural sensitivity and a global perspective are vital in today's multicultural world. A speaker who acknowledges and embraces this diversity not only avoids potential missteps but also enriches their connection with the audience. It's a respectful and insightful approach that makes for more powerful and meaningful communication.

Speaker's Canvas Relation: The Role of Members in the Framework

1) Why Understanding the Role of Members in the Framework is Important

Members, or the audience, are not passive receptors but active participants in the communication process. In the 7 Ms speaker's canvas, understanding the role of Members bridges the gap between the speaker and the audience, creating a dialogue rather than a monologue. It emphasizes that successful speaking is not merely about what the speaker wants to say but about what the audience needs to hear.

2) Historical and Recent Anecdote Why Understanding the Role of Members is Important

- **Historical Anecdote**: Cicero, the great Roman orator, was known to study his audience meticulously, considering their beliefs, interests, and needs to craft his speeches. His understanding of the Members made him one of history's most effective speakers.
- **Recent Anecdote**: Oprah Winfrey's success as a communicator is partly due to her deep connection with her audience. She doesn't just speak to them; she speaks with them, making them feel seen and heard.

3) Relating it to the Speaker's Canvas

In the 7 Ms speaker's canvas, the concept of Members is integral to all other components, including Messenger, Message, Medium, and more. The audience guides the speech's preparation, delivery, and evaluation, emphasizing a user-centered approach.

4) Details Discussing Key Advice or Considerations for Improving the Understanding of Members in the Framework

- **Know Your Audience**: Research their demographics, psychographics, needs, and expectations.

- **Engage Actively**: Encourage questions, feedback, and participation to make the audience part of the conversation.

- **Reflect and Adapt**: Consider audience feedback in shaping future speeches.

5) Three More Anecdotes

- **Contemporary**: TED Talks often begin with an understanding of the Members, framing complex ideas in accessible ways for a diverse global audience.

- **Historical Figure**: Winston Churchill's speeches during World War II were masterful in understanding the mood and needs of the British people.

- **Historical Figure**: Martin Luther King, Jr.'s "I Have a Dream" speech resonated because he spoke to the shared hopes and values of his audience.

6) Practical Advice How the User Can Improve Their Understanding of Members

- **Use Surveys or Pre-Assessment**: Get insights into the audience's background and expectations beforehand.

- **Be Present**: Engage with the audience before and after the speech to create a more personal connection.

- **Evaluate Success through Feedback**: Post-speech feedback from the audience can help refine future performances.

7) Conclusion

The role of Members in the 7 Ms speaker's canvas is central to the entire speaking process. Recognizing that the audience is at the heart of every successful speech fosters a more participatory, engaging, and effective communication process. It's a philosophy that turns speakers into listeners, ensuring that their words truly resonate.

Body Language & Non-Verbal Communication: Reading Audience Cues

1) Why Understanding Body Language and Non-Verbal Communication is Important

Communication is not solely about words. Body language and non-verbal cues often convey more than what is being said. A skilled speaker reads the audience's body language to gauge their engagement, understanding, and feelings, and adapts accordingly. This unspoken connection adds depth and dimension to the communication process.

2) Historical and Recent Anecdote Why Understanding Body Language and Non-Verbal Communication is Important

- **Historical Anecdote**: Margaret Thatcher, Britain's first female Prime Minister, understood the power of non-verbal communication. Her deliberate control of her voice, posture, and gestures contributed to her commanding presence.
- **Recent Anecdote**: Tony Robbins, the motivational speaker, is adept at reading his audience's body language and energy. His ability to connect non-verbally contributes to his dynamic and engaging presentations.

3) Relating it to the Speaker's Canvas

Within the 7 Ms speaker's canvas, body language falls under Members as it's about understanding and responding to the audience's non-verbal cues. It's an essential aspect of Monitoring, too, as speakers must continually gauge and adjust to audience reactions.

4) Details Discussing Key Advice or Considerations for Improving Understanding of Body Language

- **Learn to Recognize Common Cues**: For instance, crossed arms may indicate resistance, while leaning forward might suggest interest.

- **Use Your Body Language**: Convey confidence and passion through your posture, gestures, and facial expressions.

- **Respond to Audience Cues**: If you notice signs of confusion or disengagement, be prepared to clarify or reengage the audience.

5) Three More Anecdotes

- **Contemporary**: Brene Brown's ability to connect through authenticity is evident in her TED Talk, where her expressive body language complements her message on vulnerability.

- **Historical Figure**: Adolf Hitler manipulated body language to stir emotions in his speeches, a dark reminder of how powerful non-verbal communication can be.
- **Historical Figure**: Mahatma Gandhi's humble and gentle non-verbal demeanor communicated a profound message of peace and non-violence.

6) Practical Advice How the User Can Improve Their Understanding of Body Language

- **Practice with a Mentor**: Work with someone experienced in non-verbal communication to develop this skill.

- **Use Mirroring**: Subtly reflecting the audience's body language can create rapport.

- **Record and Review**: Watching recordings of your speeches can reveal both your non-verbal strengths and areas for improvement.

7) Conclusion

Body language and non-verbal communication are silent yet potent aspects of public speaking. Understanding and utilizing these cues enhance the connection between speaker and audience, adding depth and responsiveness to the spoken word. The ability to read and respond to these unspoken signals is an art that, when mastered, can elevate your speaking to new heights.

Detailed Discussion: Strategies for Engaging Members

1) Why Understanding Strategies for Engaging Members is Important

Audience engagement is the core of effective public speaking. A speech that fails to engage is like a song sung to an empty room. Thus, employing strategies to keep the audience involved, curious, and responsive is paramount for the speaker's success.

2) Historical and Recent Anecdote Why Understanding Strategies for Engaging Members is Important

- **Historical Anecdote**: Socrates, with his Socratic method, engaged his audiences through questioning and dialogue rather than lecturing, sparking critical thinking and participation.

- **Recent Anecdote**: Steve Jobs, in his iconic product launches, used storytelling, visuals, and suspense to keep audiences riveted.

3) Relating it to the Speaker's Canvas

Engagement strategies are woven throughout the 7 Ms speaker's canvas, especially in Members (audience), Message (content), and Medium (delivery). Integrating these elements creates a synergistic effect that holds the audience's attention.

4) Details Discussing Key Advice or Considerations for Engaging Members

- **Start with a Bang**: Use a gripping story, startling fact, or provocative question to hook the audience.

- **Use Visual Aids**: Images, charts, or videos can enhance understanding and interest.

- **Interact**: Ask questions, conduct polls, or invite audience participation to break the monologue.

5) Three More Anecdotes

- **Contemporary**: Simon Sinek's "Start with Why" talk engages by turning conventional thinking upside down, making the audience think differently.

- **Historical Figure**: Susan B. Anthony engaged her audiences on women's rights by linking the struggle to familiar concepts like freedom and equality.

- **Historical Figure**: Franklin D. Roosevelt's fireside chats engaged listeners by speaking to them as if they were in the same room, building trust and connection.

6) Practical Advice How the User Can Improve Engagement with Members

- **Know Your Audience**: Tailor content to their interests, needs, and level of understanding.

- **Use Varied Tone and Pace**: Modulate your voice to maintain interest and emphasize key points.

- **Provide Takeaways**: Summarize key points and offer actionable insights for the audience to ponder and apply.

7) Conclusion

Engaging members is both an art and a science, encompassing everything from content creation to delivery. It requires a deep understanding of the audience and a willingness to connect on an intellectual and emotional level. Whether through stories, visuals, or interactive elements, effective engagement turns a speech from a monologue into a dynamic dialogue, leaving a lasting impact.

Adaptation & Flexibility: Adjusting to Audience Feedback

1) Why Adaptation and Flexibility are Important

Adaptation and flexibility in public speaking reflect a speaker's ability to respond in real-time to the audience's reactions and feedback. It's the willingness to depart from a script if it means better connecting with the audience. In a world where no two audiences are the same, this skill is crucial.

2) Historical and Recent Anecdote Why Adaptation and Flexibility are Important

- **Historical Anecdote**: John F. Kennedy's improvisation during his "Ich bin ein Berliner" speech in 1963, reflecting his connection with the crowd, turned it into a historic moment.
- **Recent Anecdote**: When a TED Talk technical failure occurred, speaker Tim Harford turned the mishap into a part of his talk on embracing chaos, demonstrating impressive adaptability.

3) Relating it to the Speaker's Canvas

In the 7 Ms speaker's canvas, adaptation aligns closely with Monitoring and Members, requiring continuous reading of the audience and adjusting the Message and Medium as needed. It's a dynamic process that keeps a speech alive and relevant.

4) Details Discussing Key Advice or Considerations for Improving Adaptation and Flexibility

- **Be Present**: Stay attuned to the audience's reactions and be willing to adjust.

- **Prepare for the Unexpected**: Have backup plans or alternative examples ready.

- **Embrace Mistakes**: If something goes awry, use it as a learning opportunity or even a part of the speech.

5) Three More Anecdotes

- **Contemporary**: When Michelle Obama's teleprompter failed, she smoothly continued her speech, showcasing her adaptability.

- **Historical Figure**: Abraham Lincoln was known to adjust his speeches according to audience reactions, even changing his stance on key issues.

- **Historical Figure**: Winston Churchill would alter his speeches on the fly, even changing entire sections to suit the audience's mood.

6) Practical Advice How the User Can Improve Adaptation and Flexibility

- **Practice with Different Audiences**: This can help you become more comfortable with varying reactions and needs.

- **Learn to Read Cues**: Understand both verbal and non-verbal cues to gauge when adjustments are needed.
- **Don't Over-Script**: Leave room in your preparation for spontaneity and adaptation.

7) Conclusion

Adaptation and flexibility transform public speaking from a static performance into a dynamic interaction. By being willing to change course, respond to unexpected circumstances, and meet the audience where they are, you breathe life into your words. It turns speaking from a rehearsed act into an art form, where the unexpected becomes an opportunity rather than an obstacle.

Practical Advice: Improving Audience Engagement

1) Why Improving Audience Engagement is Important

Audience engagement is the heartbeat of any speech. If the audience is disinterested or disconnected, even the most eloquent speech will fall flat. Improving engagement is not just about holding attention; it's about making a lasting impression, influencing thoughts, and inspiring action.

2) Historical and Recent Anecdote Why Improving Audience Engagement is Important

- **Historical Anecdote**: Martin Luther King Jr.'s "I Have a Dream" speech is a prime example of engaging an audience so profoundly that it becomes a catalyst for social change.

- **Recent Anecdote**: TED speaker Sir Ken Robinson engaged his audience with humor and relatable insights, making his talk on education one of the most viewed ever.

3) Relating it to the Speaker's Canvas

The 7 Ms speaker's canvas considers Members (audience) central to the entire process. Engagement intertwines with every other 'M,' especially Message (what you're saying) and Medium (how you're saying it). They must all align to create an engaging experience.

4) Details Discussing Key Advice or Considerations for Improving Audience Engagement

- **Create a Narrative**: Stories humanize content, making it accessible and memorable.

- **Use Props or Visuals**: These can enhance understanding and keep attention.

- **Ask Thought-Provoking Questions**: This encourages active listening and participation.

5) Three More Anecdotes

- **Contemporary**: Elon Musk's product launches use visuals, demos, and anticipation to engage.

- **Historical Figure**: Cicero, the Roman orator, mastered rhetorical questions to engage his listeners.

- **Historical Figure**: Former President Bill Clinton's ability to make each audience member feel spoken to was a cornerstone of his engagement strategy.

6) Practical Advice How the User Can Improve Audience Engagement

- **Know Your Audience's Needs**: Speak to what matters to them.

- **Build Energy and Enthusiasm**: Your passion can ignite theirs.

- **Provide Actionable Takeaways**: Give them something of value to apply or think about.

7) Conclusion

Improving audience engagement is not a formula but an ongoing relationship with those you're speaking to. It requires empathy, creativity, responsiveness, and a willingness to see the audience not as mere recipients but as active participants in a shared journey. By focusing on engagement, you're not just talking at people; you're communicating with them, making your words resonate long after the speech ends.

Conclusion: Reflection and Evaluation & Feedback on Engaging Members

Understanding and engaging your audience, or the 'Members' in the 7 Ms framework, is perhaps one of the most vital aspects of public speaking. From emotional connection and cultural sensitivity to non-verbal communication, adaptation, and practical engagement strategies, we have journeyed through the multifaceted landscape of audience interaction.

In embracing these insights, you don't just become a speaker but a communicator, able to connect with different people in various contexts. The art of engaging with members is an ever-evolving dance, filled with nuances and opportunities for growth.

By reflecting on your engagements and seeking feedback, you can continue to refine and deepen these connections. Whether you are an aspiring public speaker or a seasoned orator, the path to mastering audience engagement is an endless yet rewarding journey.

Bibliography

1. Carnegie, D. (1936). "How to Win Friends and Influence People." Simon & Schuster.
2. Cialdini, R. B. (1984). "Influence: The Psychology of Persuasion." Harper Business.
3. Gladwell, M. (2000). "The Tipping Point: How Little Things Can Make a Big Difference." Little, Brown and Company.
4. Sinek, S. (2009). "Start with Why: How Great Leaders Inspire Everyone to Take Action." Portfolio.

5. Zimbardo, P., & Leippe, M. (1991). "The Psychology of Attitude Change and Social Influence." McGraw-Hill.

Recommended Reading
1. Brown, B. (2012). "Daring Greatly: How the Courage to Be Vulnerable Transforms the Way We Live, Love, Parent, and Lead." Gotham Books.
2. Duarte, N. (2010). "Resonate: Present Visual Stories that Transform Audiences." Wiley.
3. Humes, J. C. (2008). "Speak Like Churchill, Stand Like Lincoln: 21 Powerful Secrets of History's Greatest Speakers." Three Rivers Press.

By weaving the ideas, strategies, and examples explored in this chapter into your public speaking practice, you stand to not only improve your skills but to make a lasting impact on those you address.

Chapter 2: The Messenger

Introduction: Why the Messenger is Vital

The role of the messenger, or speaker, in public speaking cannot be understated. They are the human conduit that brings the message to life, crafting the words and sentiments into a form that can ignite the minds and hearts of the audience. Without the messenger, the words remain mere ink on paper. It's the messenger who breathes life into them, giving them shape, rhythm, and resonance.

Why is the Messenger Important?

The messenger acts as a bridge between the idea and the listener. They are the living embodiment of the message, translating abstract concepts into palpable emotions and tangible examples. Their voice, their tone, their body language - all of these contribute to how the message is received.

Historical Anecdote: Cicero's Oratory

Consider the Roman statesman Cicero, one of history's greatest orators. Cicero didn't merely speak to his audience; he engaged them, stirred them, and won them over with his eloquence and passion. When he spoke against Catiline in the Senate, he didn't just lay out the facts; he painted a vivid picture of the danger that Catiline posed, using rhetorical flourish and emotional appeal. Cicero was not just a conveyor of information; he was a performer, an artist, and his words were his canvas.

Recent Anecdote: Malala Yousafzai's Speeches

Fast forward to the modern age, and we find Malala Yousafzai, a young Pakistani activist who stood up for education and women's rights in her country. Malala's speeches are not only powerful in content but in delivery. When she addresses the world, she speaks from her heart, and her words resonate with a sincerity that captivates listeners. Her courage and conviction shine through her words, making her message not just heard but felt.

Relating it to the Speaker's Canvas

In the framework of the 7 Ms, the messenger is the human element that touches the listener's soul. They're the guide leading the audience through the labyrinth of ideas, breaking down complex thoughts into digestible pieces, and connecting on a level that transcends mere information. The messenger is more than a voice; they are the heart, soul, and face of the message.

Key Advice for Realizing the Importance of the Messenger

1. **Embrace Your Uniqueness:** Your voice is unique, and it's your most powerful tool. Don't try to mimic others; instead, find your authentic voice and embrace it.

2. **Connect with Your Audience:** Understand who you're speaking to and what they need. Speak to their hearts, not just their minds.

3. **Practice and Refine:** Being a great messenger requires practice and refinement. Keep honing your skills, seeking feedback, and growing.

4. **Use Your Body, Not Just Your Words:** Remember, communication isn't just verbal. Your body language, your eyes, your gestures - all these play a part in how your message is received.

Conclusion

The messenger is the soul of any speech. They are the ones who make the words dance, the ideas sing, and the message resonate in the hearts of the listeners. In the world of public speaking, content is essential, but it's the messenger that gives it wings. And like the skilled artist Cicero or the passionate activist Malala, the true power of a messenger lies in their ability to connect, inspire, and transform.

Emotional Intelligence & Connection: Building Rapport

Emotional intelligence is a vital skill for a public speaker. It's about understanding and managing not only your own emotions but also those of your audience. By connecting with the audience emotionally, a speaker can build rapport, foster trust, and create a lasting impact.

Why Emotional Intelligence is Key

Emotional intelligence allows a speaker to read the room, gauge the mood of the audience, and adapt the message accordingly. It helps the speaker to empathize with the listeners, to see things from their perspective, and to shape the speech in a way that resonates with them.

Historical Anecdote: Franklin D. Roosevelt's Fireside Chats

During the Great Depression, President Franklin D. Roosevelt used his "Fireside Chats" to speak directly to the American people. Roosevelt's ability to connect on an emotional level, to speak as a friend and a fellow citizen rather than a distant President, helped him build rapport with the listeners. People felt that Roosevelt understood their fears and worries. This emotional connection made his messages more effective and enduring.

Recent Anecdote: Brené Brown's Talks on Vulnerability

Brené Brown, a research professor, and public speaker, has won millions of hearts with her talks on vulnerability and courage. Brown's ability to speak openly about her own experiences and emotions allows her to connect with the audience on a deeply personal level. She doesn't just discuss theories; she shares her own life, making her words relatable and real.

Relating it to the Speaker's Canvas

In the framework of the 7 Ms, emotional intelligence and connection tie into the "Messenger" by enhancing the speaker's ability to connect on a deeper level. It's about building a bridge between the speaker's heart and the audience's, making the message not just heard but felt.

Key Advice for Building Rapport through Emotional Intelligence

1. **Know Your Audience:** Understanding the needs, values, and emotions of your audience helps in crafting a message that resonates with them.

2. **Be Authentic:** Authenticity fosters trust. Share real stories, show genuine emotions, and be yourself on stage.

3. **Use Empathy:** Put yourself in the shoes of your listeners. What are they feeling? What do they need to hear? Speaking to those emotions will create a deeper connection.

4. **Adapt Your Message:** Be flexible and responsive to the mood of the room. If something's not working, don't be afraid to change course.

Conclusion

Emotional intelligence is not just a business buzzword; it's a foundational skill for anyone looking to communicate effectively. From Roosevelt's calming reassurances during dark times to Brené Brown's heartfelt talks on vulnerability, the ability to connect emotionally turns a speech from mere words into a powerful connection. It's the magic that turns a speaker into a messenger, a person who doesn't just talk but reaches into the hearts of the listeners.

By nurturing emotional intelligence, embracing authenticity, and practicing empathy, you can become a messenger who doesn't just speak but connects. And in the world of public speaking, that connection is everything.

Anecdotes: Historical and Recent Examples of Effective Messengers

Anecdotes are the spices of storytelling, enriching the flavor and adding depth. They make abstract concepts tangible and dry facts memorable. Through stories, we can connect with history, learn from it, and see ourselves in the reflection of those who've walked before us.

Historical: Winston Churchill's Ability to Inspire

Sir Winston Churchill, Britain's wartime Prime Minister, is an icon of persuasive and inspirational speaking. During the dark days of World War II, when Britain stood on the brink of invasion, Churchill didn't mince words. He spoke bluntly of the hardships ahead but infused his speeches with an unbreakable spirit.
His most famous speech, "We Shall Fight on the Beaches," is a masterpiece of rhetoric and emotion. Churchill's words were not just an update on the war; they were a rallying cry, a call to arms, a poetic painting of defiance and resilience. His ability to articulate the emotions of an entire nation turned his speeches into beacons of hope in a time of despair.

Recent: Oprah Winfrey's Connective Speaking Style

Oprah Winfrey, the media mogul, and philanthropist has a unique ability to connect with people from all walks of life. Whether interviewing a celebrity or a common person, Oprah's style of speaking is intimate and empathetic. She listens as much as she talks and makes people feel seen and heard.

Her speech at the 2018 Golden Globes, where she spoke about justice, equality, and hope, was a testament to her power as a messenger. She didn't just deliver a speech; she told a story, a narrative that wove history, personal experiences, and universal truths into a tapestry that touched hearts around the world.

Relating it to the Speaker's Canvas

In the 7 Ms framework, anecdotes serve as the narrative threads that bind the entire speech together. They are tools that the messenger uses to make the message more accessible, more human. Anecdotes are bridges that link the speaker's world to that of the audience, allowing them to travel together on a journey of understanding.

Key Advice for Using Anecdotes Effectively

1. **Make it Relevant:** Choose anecdotes that align with your message and resonate with your audience.

2. **Tell it Well:** An anecdote is a mini-story. Craft it with a beginning, middle, and end. Use descriptive language to paint a vivid picture.

3. **Connect Emotionally:** The best anecdotes touch the heart. Share stories that evoke empathy, joy, surprise, or any emotion that serves your message.

4. **Be Authentic:** Share personal stories if they are relevant. Authenticity creates a stronger connection.

Conclusion

Anecdotes are more than decorative flourishes; they are essential tools in the arsenal of an effective messenger. From Churchill's rallying cries to Oprah's heartfelt narratives, anecdotes have the power to turn a speech into an experience, a moment that stays with the listener long after the words have faded.

In your journey as a messenger, embrace the art of storytelling. Use anecdotes to breathe life into your speech, to make it more than a collection of facts and arguments. Let your stories be the heartbeat of your message, and you'll not only speak to the minds of your audience but to their souls.

Storytelling & Narrative Structure: Crafting Personal Narratives

Storytelling is an ancient and powerful tool that has been used to communicate ideas, share wisdom, and connect with others. When it comes to public speaking, crafting personal narratives through storytelling can transform an ordinary speech into an extraordinary experience.

Why Storytelling Matters in Public Speaking

We are wired for stories. Our brains respond to narratives in a way that they don't to cold facts and statistics. Stories are relatable, memorable, and emotional. They allow the speaker to take the audience on a journey, making complex ideas more accessible and engaging.

Historical Anecdote: Abraham Lincoln's Use of Stories

Abraham Lincoln, one of America's greatest orators, was known for his skill in storytelling. Whether in debates or speeches, Lincoln often used simple, down-to-earth anecdotes to make his points. These stories were not just entertaining; they were strategically crafted to convey complex political ideas in a way that was easy to grasp.

In his Cooper Union speech, Lincoln used the narrative structure to lay out his arguments against slavery, weaving historical facts into a compelling story that resonated with his audience.

Recent Anecdote: Malala Yousafzai's Personal Story of Courage

Malala Yousafzai, the young Pakistani education activist, uses her personal story to advocate for girls' education worldwide. Shot by the Taliban for attending school,

Malala's story is not just a tale of survival but a testament to courage, resilience, and the power of education.

Her speeches are filled with personal narratives, connecting her life's journey to the broader issue of girls' education. Her storytelling makes her message more powerful, turning statistics about education into a human story that touches hearts.

Relating it to the Speaker's Canvas

In the context of the 7 Ms, storytelling and narrative structure are essential components of the "Messenger." Crafting personal narratives enables the speaker to become a character in the speech, inviting the audience into a shared experience. It creates a deeper connection between the messenger and the listeners.

Key Advice for Crafting Personal Narratives

1. **Know Your Audience:** Tailor your story to resonate with your listeners, using themes and values that they can relate to.

2. **Build a Structure:** Like any good story, a personal narrative needs a beginning, middle, and end. Introduce the characters, build tension, and deliver a resolution.

3. **Use Imagery and Emotions:** Paint pictures with your words, make your audience see, feel, and experience the story.

4. **Relate it to Your Message:** Ensure that the story aligns with the core message of your speech. It should enhance, not distract from your key points.

Conclusion

Storytelling is not just a skill; it's an art. From Lincoln's skillful use of anecdotes to Malala's inspiring personal journey, storytelling has the power to transform speeches from mere words into living, breathing narratives.

As you craft your speeches, embrace the art of storytelling. Let your personal narratives be the vehicle through which you connect, engage, and inspire your audience. Remember, people may forget what you said, but they will never forget how you made them feel.

Whether you are advocating for a cause, inspiring change, or sharing wisdom, let your story be the heart of your message. In the world of public speaking, a well-told story is worth more than a thousand facts.

Body Language & Non-Verbal Communication: Enhancing Presence

In the art of public speaking, what you say is crucial, but how you say it is equally significant. Body language and non-verbal communication play a vital role in conveying your message and connecting with your audience.

Why Body Language Matters

Communication is more than just words. Our body language, facial expressions, and tone of voice convey subtle messages that can either reinforce or undermine what we are saying. An engaging speaker knows how to use non-verbal cues to enhance their presence and create a more impactful experience for the audience.

Historical Anecdote: Martin Luther King Jr.'s Charismatic Presence

Dr. Martin Luther King Jr.'s "I Have a Dream" speech is not only famous for its powerful words but also for King's charismatic delivery. His body language was expressive, filled with conviction and passion. He used hand gestures to emphasize key points and maintained eye contact to connect with his listeners.

His posture, tone, and expressions were all in harmony with his message of hope and equality. It's a timeless example of how non-verbal communication can amplify the impact of a speech.

Recent Anecdote: TED Speaker Amy Cuddy's Research on Power Poses

Amy Cuddy's TED Talk on power poses has become one of the most-watched talks in TED's history. Cuddy, a social psychologist, shares her research on how our body language affects how others see us and even how we see ourselves.
Her own presentation is a living example of her research. She embodies her message through confident body

language, engaging gestures, and a warm, authentic presence.

Relating it to the Speaker's Canvas

In the framework of the 7 Ms, body language and non-verbal communication are integral to the "Messenger." They are the visual and auditory expressions of the message, the unspoken words that can make or break a speech.

Key Advice for Enhancing Presence through Body Language

1. **Be Mindful of Your Posture:** Stand tall and confident. Good posture not only looks assertive but makes you feel more confident.

2. **Use Gestures Wisely:** Hand gestures can emphasize points, but don't overdo it. Find a natural rhythm that complements your words.

3. **Maintain Eye Contact:** Eye contact creates a personal connection. Look at different sections of the audience to make everyone feel included.

4. **Express Emotion Through Facial Expressions:** Your face conveys emotions. Let it reflect what you're feeling and saying.

5. **Control Your Voice:** Vary your tone, pitch, and pace to keep the audience engaged. Your voice is a powerful instrument; use it to its fullest.

Conclusion

Body language and non-verbal communication are the unsung heroes of effective public speaking. From Martin Luther King Jr.'s inspiring presence to Amy Cuddy's embodiment of her research, the way we use our body and voice can elevate our message and create a lasting impact.

As you develop your skills as a messenger, pay attention to your non-verbal cues. Practice in front of a mirror or record yourself to see how you come across. Remember, your body speaks even when you're silent. Let it speak in harmony with your words, and you will not only be heard but felt and remembered.

Detailed Discussion: Key Advice for Effectiveness

Becoming an effective messenger involves a blend of many elements. It's not just about what you say but how you say it.

Here are some vital insights and tips that can elevate your effectiveness as a speaker:

1. Authenticity is Key:

- **Be Yourself:** Authenticity creates trust. Embrace your unique voice and style, and don't try to imitate others.
- **Speak from the Heart:** Share what you genuinely believe in. Passion shines through and can be contagious.

2. Clarity and Simplicity:

- **Be Clear:** Use straightforward language. Avoid jargon and complex sentences that can lose your audience.
- **Repeat Key Points:** Reinforcement helps in retention. Summarize your main points throughout the speech.

3. Engage Your Audience:

- **Ask Questions:** Interaction keeps listeners engaged. Pose rhetorical or actual questions to provoke thought.
- **Use Humor When Appropriate:** A well-placed joke can lighten the mood and make you more relatable.

4. Prepare and Practice:

- **Know Your Material:** Confidence comes from preparation. Know your content inside and out.
- **Rehearse:** Practice makes perfect. Rehearse multiple times to feel at ease with your delivery.

6. Handle Challenges Gracefully:

- **Manage Interruptions:** Be prepared for unexpected questions or interruptions. Stay calm and handle them with poise.
- **Adapt to Technical Issues:** Technology can fail. Have a backup plan and remain composed if things go awry.

6. Use Visual Aids Effectively:

- **Enhance, Don't Distract:** Visual aids should support your message, not take the focus away from it.
- **Test in Advance:** Ensure that all equipment is working before you start.

7. Reflect and Grow:

- **Seek Feedback:** Constructive criticism helps you grow. Welcome it and learn from it.
- **Reflect on Your Performance:** After each speech, think about what went well and what you can improve.

Conclusion:

Becoming an effective messenger is an ongoing journey. It requires a blend of authenticity, clarity, engagement, preparation, adaptability, visual prowess, and reflection. Remember the timeless wisdom of Winston Churchill, who once said, "If you have an important point to make, don't try to be subtle or clever. Use a pile driver. Hit the point once. Then come back and hit it again. Then hit it a third time - a tremendous whack."

Your effectiveness as a messenger is not just about delivering information; it's about making an impact. It's about resonating with your audience, leaving them with something that lingers long after your speech has ended.

Rhetorical Techniques: Mastering Persuasive Speech

Persuasion is at the heart of public speaking. Whether you're trying to inspire, inform, entertain, or convince, using rhetorical techniques can greatly enhance your message's impact. Understanding these techniques and how to employ them effectively can set you apart as a masterful messenger.

1. Ethos: Building Credibility

- **Show Your Expertise:** Establish your credibility by demonstrating your knowledge and experience in the subject matter.
- **Share Your Values:** Connect with your audience by showing that you share common values and beliefs.

2. Pathos: Appealing to Emotion

- **Tell Emotional Stories:** Narratives that tug at the heartstrings can create a strong emotional connection.
- **Use Vivid Language:** Descriptive language can paint a picture in the listener's mind, invoking strong feelings.

4. Logos: Logical Appeal

- **Present Facts and Statistics:** Concrete evidence adds weight to your argument.
- **Use Logical Reasoning:** Build a well-structured argument that leads your audience to the desired conclusion.

4. The Art of Repetition

- **Anaphora:** Repeating the same word or phrase at the beginning of successive sentences, as seen in Martin Luther King Jr.'s "I have a dream" speech.
- **Epistrophe:** Repeating the same word or phrase at the end of successive sentences, emphasizing a particular point.

5. Rhetorical Questions

- **Provoke Thought:** Asking questions without expecting an answer can encourage the audience to reflect on the topic.

6. Metaphors and Similes

- **Create Connections:** Comparing unrelated things through metaphor or simile can create powerful imagery and enhance understanding.

7. Triads: The Rule of Three

- **Harness the Power of Three:** Listing three related items or ideas is more engaging and memorable, such as "Life, Liberty, and the Pursuit of Happiness."

Historical Example: Cicero's Oratory Skills

Cicero, the ancient Roman philosopher, was renowned for his persuasive oratory. He employed these rhetorical techniques masterfully, weaving ethos, pathos, and logos into his speeches, which are still studied today.

Contemporary Example: Barack Obama's Speeches

Former President Barack Obama is known for his eloquent use of rhetorical devices. His speeches often include repetition, vivid imagery, and emotional appeal, making him one of the most compelling modern orators.

Conclusion:

Rhetorical techniques are powerful tools in a speaker's arsenal. They are the fine brushes that add texture and depth to the canvas of your speech. Whether it's the ethical appeal of ethos, the emotional tug of pathos, the logical structure of logos, or the creative use of language, mastering these techniques will enable you to craft persuasive and memorable speeches.

As you continue to grow as a messenger, explore these techniques. Experiment with them in your speeches. Watch how they can transform your message from ordinary to extraordinary.

Adaptation & Flexibility: Adapting to Different Audiences

The ability to adapt your message and delivery style to different audiences is a vital skill for a speaker. Understanding who you're speaking to, what they care about, and how they perceive information can dramatically affect the success of your communication.

1. Know Your Audience:

- **Demographics:** Consider age, gender, cultural background, profession, and interests.
- **Understanding Expectations:** Know what your audience is hoping to gain from your speech.
- **Identify Common Ground:** Find shared values or interests to create a connection.

2. Adapt Your Language and Tone:

- **Technical vs. Non-Technical:** Adjust your language based on the audience's familiarity with the subject.
- **Formal vs. Informal:** Choose a tone that fits the setting and the audience's expectations.

3. Customize Content:

- **Relevance:** Highlight points that are most pertinent to the audience.
- **Use Appropriate Examples and Analogies:** Tailor examples that resonate with the audience's background.

4. Consider Cultural Sensitivities:

- **Respect Differences:** Recognize and respect cultural norms and values.
- **Avoid Potential Pitfalls:** Steer clear of humor or references that may be inappropriate or offensive.

Historical Anecdote: Franklin D. Roosevelt's Fireside Chats

During the Great Depression, President Franklin D. Roosevelt used radio to speak directly to the American people. He adjusted his language and content to connect with ordinary citizens, using plain language and simple metaphors to explain complex economic and political issues. This approach made him accessible and relatable to a broad audience.

Recent Example: Steve Jobs's Product Presentations

Steve Jobs was a master at adapting his presentations to his audience. Whether addressing tech experts, business people, or everyday consumers, he knew how to present Apple's products in a way that spoke to each group's specific interests and needs. His ability to tune his message to different audiences was a key factor in his extraordinary success as a presenter.

Speaker's Canvas Relation: The Messenger's Role in Adapting

In the 7 Ms framework, adaptation is a core aspect of the "Messenger." Recognizing the needs and expectations of your audience, and being flexible enough to tailor your message accordingly, is an essential quality of an effective messenger.

Conclusion:

Adapting to different audiences isn't just about changing what you say; it's about understanding and connecting with the people you're speaking to. It's about empathy, respect, and a willingness to meet your audience where they are.

From Roosevelt's fireside chats to Steve Jobs's iconic product launches, the ability to adapt is a hallmark of great communicators.

As you develop your skills as a messenger, always keep your audience in mind. They're not just passive listeners; they're active participants in the communication process. Your ability to adapt and connect with them will not only make your message more impactful but also turn your speech into a shared experience.

Practical Advice: Improving as the Messenger

Becoming an effective messenger is a journey, and like any worthwhile journey, it requires practice, reflection, and a willingness to grow. Here's some hands-on advice that will help you become not just a good speaker but a great one.

1. Practice, Practice, Practice:

- **Rehearse Your Speech:** Even the most seasoned speakers rehearse. It builds confidence and helps in refining your delivery.
- **Record Yourself:** Watching a recording can reveal areas for improvement in tone, body language, and pace.

2. Seek Feedback:

- **Find a Trusted Mentor or Peer:** Regular feedback from someone who understands your goals can be invaluable.
- **Join a Speaking Group:** Organizations like Toastmasters offer supportive environments to practice and improve.

3. Work on Your Presence:

- **Develop Your Voice:** Your voice is an instrument. Learn how to use pitch, tone, and pace to your advantage.
- **Focus on Body Language:** Your physical presence says a lot. Use gestures and movement to reinforce your message.

4. Personalize Your Speech:

- **Use Personal Stories:** Sharing your experiences makes your speech more relatable and engaging.
- **Customize for Your Audience:** As discussed earlier, adapt your content and style to the audience's needs and expectations.

5. Embrace Technology:

- **Use Tools to Enhance Your Presentation:** Slides, videos, or other visuals can add depth to your speech.
- **Stay Up-to-Date:** Technology evolves, so keep an eye on new tools and platforms that can enhance your speaking abilities.
-

6. Learn from Others:

- **Watch Great Speakers:** Learn by observing how others connect, engage, and inspire.
- **Read Widely:** Books on public speaking, like Dale Carnegie's "The Art of Public Speaking," offer time-tested wisdom.

7. Stay True to Yourself:

- **Find Your Unique Style:** Don't try to be someone else. Embrace your individuality and speak with authenticity.
- **Enjoy the Process:** Speaking can be enjoyable and fulfilling. Find joy in connecting with others through your words.

Conclusion:

Improving as a messenger is an ongoing process, a path filled with discovery, growth, and connection. It's not about perfection but progression.

Remember the journey of Winston Churchill, who struggled with a speech impediment but went on to become one of history's most revered orators. His dedication to improvement and mastery of the craft of speaking turned a challenge into a triumph.

Whether you're speaking to a room full of executives or a classroom of curious eighth graders, the art of connecting as a messenger transcends boundaries. It's a skill that, once honed, can open doors, inspire change, and create lasting impact.

Embrace the journey, learn from each experience, and never stop growing as a messenger.

Conclusion: Evaluation & Feedback, Both Self-Evaluation and Audience Feedback

The role of a messenger doesn't end with the closing remarks of a speech. The continuous process of evaluation and feedback, both from yourself and your audience, is where growth and mastery truly flourish.

1. Self-Evaluation: Reflecting on Your Performance

- **Identify Strengths and Weaknesses:** What went well? What could have been better? Honest self-reflection is key.
- **Set Goals for Improvement:** Use your self-assessment to set achievable targets for your next speech.

2. Audience Feedback: Listening to Others

- **Solicit Feedback:** Encourage the audience to share their thoughts and impressions.
- **Analyze Feedback Thoughtfully:** Look for common themes and areas for growth.

3. Continuous Learning: Embracing Growth

- **Seek Opportunities to Speak:** The more you speak, the more you'll grow.
- **Invest in Training and Education:** Consider workshops, courses, or coaching.
-

4. Embrace Mistakes as Learning Opportunities

- **Learn from Failure:** Every mistake is a chance to learn. Embrace them as part of your journey.
- **Celebrate Progress, Not Just Perfection:** Acknowledge and celebrate small victories along the way.

Conclusion:

Being an effective messenger is more than just delivering a speech; it's an ongoing process of learning, growing, and connecting. From Winston Churchill's powerful rhetoric to Oprah Winfrey's connective style, every great messenger has a journey filled with trials, errors, victories, and constant evolution.

As you continue to develop as a messenger, remember that every speech is a new opportunity to connect, to inspire, and to grow. Cherish the process, and never stop seeking ways to improve and adapt.

Bibliography

- Carnegie, Dale. "The Art of Public Speaking."
- Gallo, Carmine. "Talk Like TED: The 9 Public-Speaking Secrets of the World's Top Minds."
- Lucas, Stephen. "The Art of Public Speaking, 12th Edition."

Recommended Reading

- "The Art of Public Speaking" by Dale Carnegie
- "Steal the Show" by Michael Port
- "Resonate: Present Visual Stories that Transform Audiences" by Nancy Duarte

Chapter 3: The Message

Introduction: Why the Message is Central

The message in any speech is the heart of communication. Imagine you are standing on a stage, with the audience eagerly anticipating your words. What is the soul of your connection with them? It's the message you are about to deliver.

Why is the message important?

A speech without a core message is like a ship without a compass. It may drift, but it lacks direction. The message is the core idea, the belief, the perspective you want to share with your audience. It's what you want them to think about, feel, or do as a result of listening to you.

Historical Anecdote: The Gettysburg Address

One of the most powerful examples of a clear, concise message in history is Abraham Lincoln's Gettysburg Address. In just 272 words, Lincoln conveyed a profound message about the principles of human equality and the importance of preserving the Union. The clarity and precision of his words have made this speech an enduring symbol of American ideals.

Recent Anecdote: Malala Yousafzai's Speech to the United Nations

In 2013, young activist Malala Yousafzai stood before the United Nations to deliver a message about education for all girls, regardless of their circumstances. Her passionate plea was not just about education; it was a message of hope, resilience, and empowerment.

Relating to the Speaker's Canvas

In the context of the 7 Ms speaker's canvas, the message is the central pillar that supports everything else. It's the foundation upon which your entire speech is built. When constructing a speech, consider the message as the main thread that weaves through all the other elements - Messenger, Medium, Monitoring, Mobilization, Members, Moment.

Emotional Intelligence & Connection: Crafting Resonant Messages

Understanding Emotional Intelligence

Emotional intelligence is about recognizing, understanding, and managing our emotions and those of others. In crafting a resonant message, it means speaking to the hearts of the listeners, not just their minds.

Crafting Resonant Messages

A resonant message connects with the audience on an emotional level. It stirs feelings, sparks thoughts, and motivates action. Think of Martin Luther King Jr.'s "I Have a Dream" speech. His words were charged with emotion, making them resonate with listeners across generations.

Historical Anecdote: Winston Churchill's "We Shall Fight on the Beaches"

During WWII, Winston Churchill delivered one of his most powerful speeches. The content was serious, but his emotional connection turned it into an uplifting call to action. It wasn't just information; it was an impassioned cry for resilience and determination.

Recent Anecdote: Greta Thunberg's Climate Change Activism

Greta Thunberg, the young climate activist, uses her speeches to stir emotion and urge action on climate change. Her strong emotional connection to her message makes it resonate with listeners worldwide, from politicians to students.

Speaker's Canvas Relation: Emotional Resonance and the 7 Ms

In the 7 Ms framework, emotional intelligence adds depth and color to the message. By understanding the emotions of your audience, you can tailor your message to resonate deeply with them, enhancing your connection.

Cultural Sensitivity & Global Perspective: Tailoring the Message

In a world that's growing closer together, understanding different cultures is paramount. You can't simply take a message that resonates in one culture and expect it to have the same impact in another. Here's where cultural sensitivity comes in.

Understanding Cultural Sensitivity

Cultural sensitivity is about recognizing and respecting differences in culture. It includes understanding the values, beliefs, customs, and behaviors of different cultural groups.

Tailoring the Message

When crafting a speech, consider who your audience is. What are their cultural backgrounds? What values resonate with them? Tailoring your message to your audience's cultural context can create a deeper connection.

Historical Anecdote: Nelson Mandela's Inaugural Speech

When Nelson Mandela became South Africa's President, he understood that his message needed to resonate with a diverse nation. His inaugural speech was a masterful blend of inclusivity and unity, tailored to a country with various ethnic and cultural backgrounds.

Recent Anecdote: The Global Fight Against COVID-19

World leaders and health organizations have tailored their messages about COVID-19 safety to various cultural contexts. Recognizing the importance of cultural nuances has helped in disseminating vital information more effectively.

Speaker's Canvas Relation: The Global Perspective in the 7 Ms

In the 7 Ms framework, understanding the cultural context adds a layer of sophistication to the message. It enables the speaker to reach the hearts and minds of a diverse audience, making the message more powerful and engaging.

Anecdotes: Historical and Contemporary Examples

Anecdotes are short, engaging stories that illuminate a point or idea. In the context of crafting a compelling message, anecdotes serve to illustrate the concept in a vivid and relatable way. They breathe life into abstract ideas, making them more tangible.

Historical Anecdote: Socrates' Teaching Methods

Socrates, the ancient Greek philosopher, often used anecdotes and parables to engage his listeners. Rather than lecturing, he asked probing questions, leading his students to profound insights. His method of using stories to teach has influenced educational practices for centuries.

Contemporary Anecdote: Steve Jobs' Stanford Commencement Speech

In his famous commencement speech at Stanford University, Steve Jobs shared three personal stories from his life. Each anecdote was carefully chosen to illustrate a specific lesson, making his message resonate with the graduates.

Using Anecdotes in Your Speeches

Anecdotes can be a powerful tool in your speaking toolkit. They provide a concrete example of an abstract concept, helping the audience connect with the message on a personal level. Whether historical or contemporary, well-chosen anecdotes add depth and color to your message.

Speaker's Canvas Relation: Anecdotes within the 7 Ms Framework

In the 7 Ms speaker's canvas, anecdotes play a vital role in fleshing out the message. By relating personal or historical stories that align with your core idea, you allow the audience to see the message in action. It's storytelling at its finest, and it helps to make the abstract concrete.

Storytelling & Narrative Structure: Memorable Messaging

The Power of Storytelling

Humans have been telling stories for millennia. Stories help us make sense of the world and our place in it. They entertain, enlighten, and engage us on a deeply emotional level. In crafting a message, using storytelling can make your speech unforgettable.

Crafting a Narrative Structure

Creating a compelling narrative structure involves having a clear beginning, middle, and end. The beginning sets the stage, the middle develops the story, and the end brings it all together in a satisfying conclusion.

Historical Anecdote: Aesop's Fables

Aesop's fables are an ancient example of storytelling with a message. Each short tale conveys a moral or lesson, presented in a way that's both engaging and memorable.

Contemporary Anecdote: J.K. Rowling's Harvard Commencement Speech

Author J.K. Rowling used storytelling in her Harvard commencement speech to share lessons from her own life. Her engaging narrative structure made her message about the benefits of failure and the importance of imagination deeply impactful.

Speaker's Canvas Relation: Narrative Structure within the 7 Ms Framework

In the context of the 7 Ms, storytelling is a technique that helps you craft a message that will linger in the audience's minds long after your speech is over. By weaving your message into a story, you engage the audience's emotions and make your point more relatable and memorable.

Speaker's Canvas Relation: Message within the 7 Ms Framework

Understanding the 7 Ms Framework

The 7 Ms framework (Messenger, Message, Medium, Monitoring, Mobilization, Members, Moment) provides a comprehensive guide to effective public speaking. The Message is central to this framework, acting as the foundation for all other elements.

The Role of the Message within the 7 Ms

The Message is not just what you say; it's what you want your audience to think, feel, or do as a result of your speech. It's the core idea that you want to share, and it informs every other aspect of your speech, from the way you deliver it (Medium) to how you engage with your audience (Monitoring and Mobilization).

Historical Anecdote: John F. Kennedy's "Moon Speech"

In his "Moon Speech," President Kennedy clearly articulated a bold message: America's commitment to landing a man on the moon. This central message influenced every part of his speech, from his passionate delivery to the way he mobilized support for the space program.

Contemporary Anecdote: TED Talks

TED Talks are renowned for their clear, compelling messages. Speakers are encouraged to focus on one central idea and explore it fully, relating all aspects of their talk back to this core message.

Practical Application: Using the 7 Ms in Your Speeches

Understanding the role of the Message within the 7 Ms framework allows you to craft speeches that are more focused, engaging, and impactful. By starting with a clear message, you can align all other aspects of your speech to support and enhance this central idea.

Technology & Innovation: Modern Tools for Conveying Messages

In the 21st century, technology plays a pivotal role in how we communicate. From social media to virtual reality, technology is reshaping the way we convey messages.

The Impact of Technology on Messaging

Technology opens up new channels for communication. It allows us to reach wider audiences and engage with them in innovative ways. Whether through a viral tweet, a compelling video, or an immersive VR experience, technology enhances our ability to connect.

Historical Anecdote: The Televised Debate between Nixon and Kennedy

In 1960, the first-ever televised presidential debate marked a turning point in political messaging. The medium of television gave viewers a chance to see the candidates in action, transforming the way politicians conveyed their messages.

Recent Anecdote: Virtual Reality in Education

Virtual Reality (VR) is being used in education to convey complex ideas in an engaging and interactive way. By immersing students in a VR environment, educators can make abstract concepts tangible, enhancing understanding and retention.

Speaker's Canvas Relation: Technology within the 7 Ms Framework

In the 7 Ms framework, technology falls under the umbrella of the Medium, but it also profoundly influences the Message itself. Understanding and leveraging technology allows speakers to craft messages that resonate with modern audiences, adding new dimensions to traditional communication.

Detailed Discussion: Enhancing Message Delivery

Understanding Your Message

To enhance message delivery, one must first have a deep understanding of the core message. What are you trying to convey? What emotions do you want to evoke? What action do you want to inspire?

Tailoring the Message to the Audience

Knowing your audience is key to enhancing your message delivery. Are they experts or novices in the subject? What are their interests and concerns? Tailoring your message to your audience's specific needs ensures that it resonates more profoundly.

Historical Anecdote: Franklin D. Roosevelt's Fireside Chats

FDR's Fireside Chats were masterful examples of tailoring the message to the audience. By speaking in a conversational tone and explaining complex issues in simple terms, Roosevelt connected with the American people during trying times.

Recent Anecdote: Social Media Influencers

Social media influencers understand their audience and tailor their messages to engage followers. They know what resonates with their audience and how to present it in a way that feels personal and authentic.

Speaker's Canvas Relation: Enhancing the Message within the 7 Ms Framework

In the context of the 7 Ms, enhancing message delivery involves aligning the Messenger, Medium, and Members with the core message. It's about creating harmony between all elements, ensuring that the message is not only heard but felt and understood.

Rhetorical Techniques: Crafting Compelling Content

The Art of Rhetoric

Rhetoric is the art of effective or persuasive speaking or writing. Utilizing rhetorical techniques can help you craft compelling content that engages and persuades your audience.

Techniques for Crafting Compelling Content

1. **Anaphora**: Repeating a word or phrase at the beginning of successive clauses. E.g., Martin Luther King's "I have a dream" speech.
2. **Metaphor**: Comparing two things without using "like" or "as." E.g., "Life is a journey."
3. **Pathos**: Appealing to emotion. E.g., Winston Churchill's wartime speeches.

Historical Anecdote: Julius Caesar's "Veni, Vidi, Vici"

Julius Caesar's famous statement, "I came, I saw, I conquered," is a masterful use of concise rhetoric. Its simplicity and rhythm made it an unforgettable declaration of victory.

Recent Anecdote: TED Talks and the Use of Rhetoric

Many TED Talk speakers skillfully use rhetorical techniques to enhance their messages. Techniques like storytelling, metaphors, and repetition help make their talks engaging and persuasive.

Speaker's Canvas Relation: Rhetoric within the 7 Ms Framework

Within the 7 Ms, rhetorical techniques are tools to enrich the Message. They add texture and depth, transforming a simple statement into a compelling narrative that engages the audience on multiple levels.

Practical Advice: Improving Messaging

Improving messaging is a vital skill for anyone looking to connect, persuade, or inspire others. Here's practical advice to help you craft messages that resonate.

Know Your Audience

Understanding your audience's needs, concerns, and interests enables you to tailor your message. Whether speaking to a group of students or industry professionals, knowing your audience ensures that your message hits the mark.

Be Clear and Concise

Avoid jargon or overly complex language. Aim for clarity and simplicity. A message that's easy to understand has a better chance of being remembered.

Use Storytelling and Anecdotes

As we've explored, stories and anecdotes breathe life into your message. They make abstract concepts tangible and engage the listener on an emotional level.

Historical Anecdote: Lincoln's Gettysburg Address

President Abraham Lincoln's Gettysburg Address was a model of clarity and brevity. In just 272 words, he conveyed a powerful message that still resonates today.

Recent Anecdote: Social Media Campaigns

Modern brands use storytelling and clarity in social media campaigns to connect with consumers. Memorable slogans and compelling stories resonate with people, leading to successful marketing efforts.

Speaker's Canvas Relation: Practical Advice within the 7 Ms Framework

Practical advice for improving messaging aligns with the 7 Ms by offering actionable strategies that can be applied across different contexts. Whether you're a novice or an experienced speaker, these tips can help you enhance your message's impact.

Conclusion: Evaluation & Feedback on the Message

Reflecting on the Message

Concluding our exploration of the Message, we recognize its centrality in effective communication. From crafting resonant narratives to utilizing modern technology, the message serves as the core around which all other elements revolve.

Evaluating Your Message

Evaluation involves reflecting on your message's effectiveness. Did it resonate with the audience? Did it inspire action? Gathering feedback from listeners can provide insights into what worked and what didn't.

Historical Anecdote: Winston Churchill's Speech Crafting

Winston Churchill spent hours crafting his speeches, seeking feedback from colleagues. He understood that evaluation and refinement were key to delivering powerful messages.

Recent Anecdote: Corporate Feedback Culture

Many modern corporations foster a culture of feedback, recognizing its value in improving communication. Regular evaluations help teams and leaders refine their messaging strategies.

Speaker's Canvas Relation: Evaluation within the 7 Ms Framework

Within the 7 Ms, evaluation is an essential part of the Monitoring component. It's a continuous process, allowing you to refine your message for greater impact in future engagements.

Bibliography & Recommended Reading (To Be Added Later)

The Bibliography and Recommended Reading sections will include various sources and additional materials for readers interested in delving deeper into the topic of messaging.

Chapter 4: The Moment

Introduction: The Importance of Timing and the Moment

Why Moment is Important

The moment is a critical aspect of public speaking, a fleeting instant that can make or break a speech. It's more than just a point in time; it's the culmination of everything that's been said and done, leading up to a pivotal opportunity. Recognizing and seizing that moment can turn an ordinary speech into a memorable and impactful one.

Historical and Recent Anecdote

1. **Historical Anecdote:** Winston Churchill, a master of timing, knew how to seize the moment. During a crucial time in World War II, he delivered his famous "We Shall Fight on the Beaches" speech. The timing was perfect, and his words resonated deeply with the people, motivating them during a dark period.

2. **Recent Anecdote:** A more contemporary example can be seen in the powerful speech given by Malala Yousafzai, the young activist fighting for girls' education. Her speech at the UN was not only inspiring but came at a critical moment in the global conversation about education and women's rights. Her timing added weight to her words, and her message was heard loud and clear.

Relating it to the Speaker's Canvas

The moment is an essential component of the 7 Ms Speaker's Canvas. It's not a static point but a dynamic element that interacts with the Messenger, Message, Medium, Monitoring, Mobilization, and Members. Understanding the moment helps to weave all these elements together, creating a harmonious and persuasive speech.

Details Discussing Key Advice

1. **Understand Your Audience:** Knowing what resonates with your audience will help you identify the perfect moment to deliver key points.

2. **Be Present:** Being fully engaged in the moment allows you to feel the energy in the room and adapt as needed.

3. **Practice Timing:** Rehearse your speech with timing in mind, ensuring that you hit key points at just the right moments.

Anecdotes

1. **Contemporary Anecdote:** At the 2015 Oscars, Patricia Arquette's acceptance speech for Best Supporting Actress became a rallying cry for wage equality. Her timing turned an acceptance speech into a powerful political statement.

2. **Historical Anecdotes:** Martin Luther King Jr.'s "I Have a Dream" speech is a timeless example of seizing the moment. Delivered during the March on

Washington in 1963, it's a masterful use of timing that still resonates today.

Practical Advice

1. **Watch for Signs:** Look for cues from your audience that they are engaged and ready for your key points.
2. **Adapt as Needed:** If something isn't working, be ready to adapt on the fly.

Conclusion

Timing and the moment are more than just chronological elements in a speech. They are opportunities to connect, inspire, and persuade. By understanding and seizing the moment, speakers can elevate their message and leave a lasting impression.

Adaptation & Flexibility: Recognizing the Right Moment

Why Recognizing the Right Moment is Important

Adaptation and flexibility in recognizing the right moment are pivotal skills for any speaker. The ability to adapt your message and style based on the audience's reaction requires a keen awareness of the room's energy, cultural context, and the global situation. Flexibility allows you to pivot your approach when needed, making your speech more relatable and impactful.

Historical and Recent Anecdote

1. **Historical Anecdote:** President Abraham Lincoln's Gettysburg Address was a mere 272 words, yet its brevity and timing were perfect. Delivered at the dedication of a soldiers' cemetery during the Civil War, Lincoln's adaptation to the somber mood turned a brief speech into a timeless dedication to human equality.

2. **Recent Anecdote:** In 2019, climate activist Greta Thunberg's impassioned plea at the United Nations captured the urgency of climate change. Her ability to adapt her message for world leaders, rather than just her peer group, created a globally resonant moment.

Relating it to the Speaker's Canvas

Recognizing the right moment is intricately tied to the other elements in the 7 Ms Speaker's Canvas. It requires understanding the Message, being attuned to the Members (audience), and using the appropriate Medium. The confluence of these factors leads to a speaker's ability to adapt and seize the moment effectively.

Details Discussing Key Advice

1. **Read the Room:** Understanding audience reactions and feedback allows for real-time adjustments.

2. **Be Flexible with Your Plan:** Even with thorough preparation, be ready to deviate from your plan to connect with your audience.

3. **Use Silence Effectively:** Sometimes, a pause can be more powerful than words. Recognize when to let your message resonate.

Anecdotes

1. **Contemporary Anecdote:** Steve Jobs, while introducing the iPhone in 2007, adeptly handled technical glitches by joking with the audience. His flexibility turned a potential disaster into an engaging moment.

2. **Historical Anecdotes:** During the Cuban Missile Crisis, President Kennedy's adaptability in his speeches and public addresses helped maintain calm and assert U.S. resolve, ultimately contributing to a peaceful resolution.

Practical Advice

1. **Prepare for the Unexpected:** Rehearse different scenarios and be ready to change course if needed.

2. **Practice Active Listening:** Engage with your audience and be responsive to their reactions.

Conclusion

Recognizing the right moment isn't just about following a script; it's about being present, adaptable, and flexible in your delivery. These skills allow you to connect with your audience on a deeper level and deliver a message that resonates long after you've left the stage.

This section focused on the critical role of adaptation and flexibility in recognizing and seizing the right moments in public speaking. By being attuned to the audience and the situation, speakers can create memorable and effective presentations.

Anecdotes: Mastering the Moment in Historical and Contemporary Context

Why Mastering the Moment is Important

Mastering the moment is the art of harnessing the power of timing to create a memorable experience for the audience. Anecdotes, both historical and contemporary, provide insight into how this mastery has shaped speeches and allowed speakers to connect with their audiences on a profound level.

Historical and Recent Anecdote

1. **Historical Anecdote:** John F. Kennedy's inaugural address in 1961 was filled with unforgettable lines. His command of the moment created lasting phrases like "Ask not what your country can do for you — ask what you can do for your country."

2. **Recent Anecdote:** At the 2020 Democratic National Convention, Michelle Obama's closing line, "It is what it is," resonated widely. Her mastery of the moment turned a simple statement into a defining comment on the political climate.

Relating it to the Speaker's Canvas

Mastering the moment connects with the 7 Ms Speaker's Canvas by aligning the Messenger, Message, Medium, Monitoring, Mobilization, Members, and the Moment itself. It's about crafting a speech that resonates with the audience while also considering timing and cultural context.

Details Discussing Key Advice

1. **Use Anecdotes Wisely:** Personal or historical anecdotes can illustrate a point, making it more memorable.

2. **Create a Build-Up:** Lead your audience to a key moment and deliver it with precision timing.

3. **Speak with Authenticity:** Authenticity helps in connecting with the audience, making the moment more impactful.

Anecdotes

1. **Contemporary Anecdote:** Elon Musk's product launches for Tesla and SpaceX are marked by his unconventional style and mastery of key moments, turning product announcements into viral phenomena.

2. **Historical Anecdotes:** Franklin D. Roosevelt's Fireside Chats were a masterful use of radio as a Medium, creating moments of connection during the Great Depression.

Practical Advice

1. **Learn from Others:** Study how great speakers have used moments to their advantage.
2. **Rehearse Key Moments:** Practicing those key moments will make you more confident in delivering them effectively.
3. **Embrace Your Style:** Your unique style can enhance the way you master moments in your speech.

Conclusion

Mastering the moment is an essential skill in public speaking that can turn a routine speech into a defining experience for the audience. By learning from historical and contemporary examples, speakers can find their own ways to create and seize these special moments.

In this section, we've explored the significance of mastering the moment in public speaking through the lens of anecdotes. From Kennedy's iconic lines to Musk's unconventional presentations, mastering the moment can leave a lasting impact.

Storytelling & Narrative Structure: Capturing Key Moments

Why Capturing Key Moments is Important

Storytelling and narrative structure are vital for capturing key moments in public speaking. A well-structured story can make complex ideas more accessible and create emotional resonance with the audience. By weaving key moments into a narrative, speakers can guide the audience through a journey that emphasizes the main message.

Historical and Recent Anecdote

1. **Historical Anecdote:** During the height of the Civil Rights Movement, Malcolm X delivered speeches that were structured as powerful narratives. He masterfully intertwined his personal experiences with broader social issues, capturing key moments that resonated with listeners.

2. **Recent Anecdote:** Brené Brown's TED Talk on vulnerability became one of the most-watched TED Talks ever. Her personal stories, seamlessly woven into a larger narrative, captured moments that struck a chord with millions.

Relating it to the Speaker's Canvas

Capturing key moments through storytelling and narrative structure fits within the 7 Ms Speaker's Canvas by aligning with the Message, Medium, and Moment. It provides a cohesive framework that can make the speech more engaging and relatable, enhancing the overall impact.

Details Discussing Key Advice

1. **Structure Your Story:** Beginning, middle, and end are essential, but also consider how to emphasize key moments that tie into your message.

2. **Use Visual Language:** Paint pictures with your words to help the audience visualize key moments.

3. **Connect with Emotion:** Emotional connection can make key moments more memorable and impactful.

Anecdotes

1. **Contemporary Anecdote:** J.K. Rowling's 2008 Harvard commencement speech used storytelling to convey the importance of failure and imagination. Her personal anecdotes were key moments that imparted wisdom in a relatable way.

2. **Historical Anecdotes:** Nelson Mandela often used stories from African folklore to underscore his points, turning traditional tales into powerful moments in his speeches.

Practical Advice

1. **Personalize Your Story:** Share personal experiences that reinforce your message, making it more authentic.

2. **Rehearse with Emphasis:** Practice emphasizing key moments in your story to ensure they stand out.

3. **Use Pauses Effectively:** A well-placed pause can accentuate a key moment, allowing it to sink in.

Conclusion

Capturing key moments through storytelling and narrative structure can make your speech more engaging, relatable, and memorable. By understanding how to weave these moments into a coherent narrative, you can lead your audience on a journey that resonates long after the speech has ended.

Speaker's Canvas Relation: The Moment's Role in the Framework

Why the Moment's Role in the Framework is Important

The Moment, as an integral part of the 7 Ms Speaker's Canvas, isn't just a singular instance in a speech; it's the culmination of all the elements working in harmony. The Moment is a synergy between the Messenger, Message, Medium, Monitoring, Mobilization, Members, and itself. Understanding how to orchestrate this synergy will lead to speeches that resonate and inspire.

Historical and Recent Anecdote

1. **Historical Anecdote:** Winston Churchill's wartime speeches are famous for their perfect timing. His profound understanding of the moment allowed him to inspire a nation in its darkest hour.

2. **Recent Anecdote:** Oprah Winfrey's 2018 Golden Globes speech created a stirring moment that resonated across the globe. By connecting her story with the broader narrative of the #MeToo movement, she created a powerful moment that reverberated far beyond the room.

Relating it to the Speaker's Canvas

The Moment's role in the Speaker's Canvas is a complex interplay between the seven components. It's the nexus where everything comes together, creating a connection between the speaker and the audience that transcends mere words. It's not just about delivering a message; it's about creating an experience.

Details Discussing Key Advice

1. **Synchronize the Elements:** Ensure that all components of the Speaker's Canvas are aligned and working together to create the desired moment.

2. **Understand Your Audience:** Recognize their needs and expectations to craft moments that resonate with them.

3. **Utilize Technology:** Employ tools that can enhance the moment, such as visual aids or engaging multimedia.

Anecdotes

1. **Contemporary Anecdote:** Tony Robbins' energetic seminars are examples of masterful synchronization of elements. His combination of language, body movement, visuals, and music creates moments that inspire transformation.

2. **Historical Anecdotes:** Martin Luther King Jr.'s "I Have a Dream" speech is a beautiful blend of passion (Messenger), content (Message), and

context (Moment), which made it one of the most memorable speeches in history.

Practical Advice

1. **Balance the Elements:** Don't overly focus on one aspect; ensure that all the elements of the 7 Ms are harmoniously integrated.

2. **Practice with Intent:** Rehearse with the focus on creating specific moments within the speech.

3. **Evaluate and Reflect:** After the speech, reflect on what went well and where improvements can be made.

Conclusion

The Moment's role within the Speaker's Canvas is central to creating speeches that not only inform but also inspire. By understanding how to integrate the various components into a harmonious whole, speakers can create profound connections with their audience and leave a lasting impact.

Rhetorical Techniques: Utilizing the Moment for Impact

Why Utilizing the Moment for Impact is Important

Rhetorical techniques help speakers emphasize key points and engage the audience. Utilizing the moment for impact involves the strategic use of rhetorical devices to heighten the audience's emotional response and enhance the message's resonance.

Historical and Recent Anecdote

1. **Historical Anecdote:** Julius Caesar's "Veni, Vidi, Vici" (I came, I saw, I conquered) is a prime example of concise rhetoric. This triumphant statement created a historical moment that resonates even today.

2. **Recent Anecdote:** In her UN speech on climate change, Greta Thunberg's repeated use of "How dare you?" created a stirring call to action. This rhetorical device emphasized her message and created a powerful moment.

Relating it to the Speaker's Canvas

Utilizing the moment within the 7 Ms Speaker's Canvas involves employing rhetorical techniques to reinforce the Message, engage the Members (audience), and amplify the impact of the Moment itself. Rhetoric isn't just ornamental; it's a strategic tool for enhancing communication.

Details Discussing Key Advice

1. **Choose the Right Technique:** Select rhetorical devices that align with your Message and the needs of your audience.

2. **Use with Purpose:** Rhetorical techniques should be used purposefully, not just for the sake of flair.

3. **Combine with Other Elements:** Integrate rhetorical techniques with storytelling, visuals, and other elements for a cohesive impact.

Anecdotes

1. **Contemporary Anecdote:** Steve Jobs' iPhone launch in 2007 was filled with rhetorical flourishes that built anticipation. His phrase, "Today, Apple is going to reinvent the phone," created a moment that defined an era.

2. **Historical Anecdotes:** Abraham Lincoln's Gettysburg Address employed parallelism ("of the people, by the people, for the people"), crafting a memorable moment in a mere 272 words.

Practical Advice

1. **Practice with Rhetoric:** Try different rhetorical techniques during practice to see what resonates best with your Message.

2. **Avoid Overuse:** Overusing rhetorical devices can diminish their impact. Use them wisely to create key moments.

3. **Analyze Great Speeches:** Learn from historical and contemporary speakers who have masterfully used rhetoric.

Conclusion

Utilizing the moment for impact through rhetorical techniques is an art that can elevate a speech from ordinary to extraordinary. By consciously selecting and integrating rhetorical devices, speakers can create moments that captivate the audience and amplify the message.

Rhetorical techniques are not merely stylistic choices but strategic tools that can create profound moments in public speaking. From Caesar's concise victory statement to Jobs' iPhone launch, these devices have shaped speeches that linger in our collective memory.

Detailed Discussion: Strategies for Maximizing the Moment

Why Maximizing the Moment is Important

Maximizing the Moment in public speaking is about making the most of every opportunity to connect with your audience and drive home your message. It's about creating those pivotal instances that resonate, inform, and inspire. A well-crafted moment can become the highlight of your speech, something your audience will remember and reflect upon.

Historical and Recent Anecdote

1. **Historical Anecdote:** During his inauguration, President John F. Kennedy seized the moment with his call to action: "Ask not what your country can do for you – ask what you can do for your country." This timeless phrase still resonates with many today.

2. **Recent Anecdote:** In 2014, Emma Watson's speech at the United Nations maximized the moment by launching the HeForShe campaign. She captured the attention of the world and initiated a conversation about gender equality.

Relating it to the Speaker's Canvas

Maximizing the Moment aligns with all aspects of the 7 Ms Speaker's Canvas. It connects with the Messenger's authenticity, amplifies the Message, leverages the Medium, requires astute Monitoring, calls for Mobilization, engages the Members, and culminates in the Moment itself.

Details Discussing Key Advice

1. **Understand Your Audience:** Know what resonates with them and craft moments that will touch them personally.

2. **Create Suspense and Surprise:** Lead the audience on a journey where the moment becomes a delightful or insightful revelation.

3. **Emphasize Key Points:** Use tone, body language, and rhetorical devices to emphasize moments that encapsulate your main message.

Anecdotes

1. **Contemporary Anecdote:** Elon Musk's presentations often include surprising moments, such as revealing a new Tesla model. These

moments create excitement and become the talk of the industry.

2. **Historical Anecdotes:** Mahatma Gandhi's peaceful protests were filled with moments that resonated with millions. His simple act of making salt defied an empire and became a symbol of resistance.

Practical Advice

1. **Plan but Be Flexible:** Plan your moments but also be prepared to seize unexpected opportunities during your speech.

2. **Use Visual Aids Effectively:** Visuals can enhance a moment, making it more vivid and memorable.

3. **Rehearse with Emotion:** Practice the way you'll perform, feeling the emotions you want to evoke during key moments.

Conclusion

Maximizing the Moment in public speaking is an art that requires understanding, planning, emotion, and execution. When done right, these moments become the soul of your speech, providing substance and inspiration.

Maximizing the moment is a nuanced and vital aspect of effective public speaking. From Kennedy's inaugural address to Watson's appeal for gender equality, moments are created that not only inform but also inspire. They stand as examples of how to utilize this aspect of the 7 Ms Speaker's Canvas for maximum effect.

Technology & Innovation: Tools to Enhance the Moment

Why Technology and Innovation are Important for Enhancing the Moment

In the digital age, technology and innovation have become essential tools for public speaking. From visuals and sound effects to live interactive sessions, technology can amplify and diversify the moments in a speech, creating rich experiences that stick in the minds of the audience.

Historical and Recent Anecdote

1. **Historical Anecdote:** The use of radio by Franklin D. Roosevelt for his "Fireside Chats" allowed him to reach millions of Americans in their homes, creating a new kind of intimate connection.

2. **Recent Anecdote:** Virtual reality (VR) presentations are now allowing speakers to create immersive experiences. For instance, climate change activists are using VR to let audiences experience the effects of global warming first-hand.

Relating it to the Speaker's Canvas

The use of technology and innovation links directly to the Medium and Moment aspects of the 7 Ms Speaker's Canvas. It empowers the Messenger to convey the Message with more authenticity and depth, helping the audience to engage and mobilize around the content.

Details Discussing Key Advice

1. **Use Technology Appropriately:** Match the technology with your Message and the needs of your audience.

2. **Experiment and Innovate:** Try new tools and methods to create unique moments.

3. **Prepare and Practice:** Technology can be unpredictable. Ensure everything works as planned by testing and rehearsing beforehand.

Anecdotes

1. **Contemporary Anecdote:** TED Talks are known for their innovative use of technology. From interactive 3D models to live musical performances, these tools are used to create engaging and memorable moments.

2. **Historical Anecdotes:** The televised debates between John F. Kennedy and Richard Nixon in 1960 showed how visual medium can affect perception. Those who listened on the radio thought Nixon won, while those who watched on television thought Kennedy won.

Practical Advice

1. **Stay Informed:** Keep up to date with the latest technology trends and innovations in public speaking.

2. **Balance with Substance:** Technology should enhance, not overshadow, the content of your speech.

3. **Embrace Flexibility:** Be ready to adapt if technology fails. Always have a backup plan.

Conclusion

Incorporating technology and innovation to enhance the moment is an exciting frontier in public speaking. It offers new avenues for connection, engagement, and inspiration but requires a thoughtful approach and meticulous preparation.

From Roosevelt's Fireside Chats to VR experiences, technology and innovation continue to reshape the landscape of public speaking. By thoughtfully integrating these tools, speakers can create moments that not only inform but also fascinate and inspire.

Practical Advice: Timing and Seizing Opportunities

Why Timing and Seizing Opportunities is Important

In public speaking, timing is everything. Knowing when to pause, when to emphasize, and when to move to the next point can make or break your speech. Seizing opportunities, whether planned or spontaneous, can create powerful connections with your audience.

Historical and Recent Anecdote

1. **Historical Anecdote:** Martin Luther King Jr.'s famous "I Have a Dream" speech was partly improvised. When singer Mahalia Jackson shouted, "Tell them about the dream, Martin!" he seized the

opportunity and delivered one of the most iconic speeches in history.

2. **Recent Anecdote:** During a technology failure at a major conference, a speaker switched to an impromptu Q&A session, turning a potential disaster into a memorable, engaging moment.

Relating it to the Speaker's Canvas

Timing and seizing opportunities correlate with Monitoring and Moment in the 7 Ms Speaker's Canvas. They involve reading the audience, adapting to the situation, and making the most of every chance to resonate with the listeners.

Details Discussing Key Advice

1. **Know Your Material Inside Out:** Confidence in your content allows you to adapt on the fly and seize unforeseen opportunities.

2. **Read the Audience:** Monitor their reactions and adjust your delivery accordingly.

3. **Practice Transitions and Pauses:** These are crucial for timing, helping to emphasize key points and give the audience time to reflect.

Anecdotes

1. **Contemporary Anecdote:** In a debate on education, a speaker skillfully used an unexpected question from the audience to segue into a key point, reinforcing her argument.

2. **Historical Anecdotes:** Winston Churchill, known for his oratory, often paused for effect, allowing his words to sink in. His timing turned simple speeches into profound experiences.

Practical Advice

1. **Prepare for the Unexpected:** Have contingency plans and be ready to pivot if needed.
2. **Use Silence Effectively:** A well-placed pause can be as powerful as words.
3. **Embrace Audience Interaction:** Be open to questions or comments; they can lead to enriching discussions.

Conclusion

Mastering timing and seizing opportunities requires practice, presence of mind, and a deep connection with your material and audience. These skills can turn an ordinary speech into an extraordinary experience.

Timing and the ability to seize opportunities have marked some of the greatest speeches in history. From King's dream to Churchill's pauses, these elements have transformed moments into milestones. By focusing on these aspects, any speaker can enhance their ability to connect and inspire.

Conclusion: Reflection and Evaluation & Feedback on Understanding the Moment

The Importance of Reflection and Evaluation

The art of public speaking is an evolving journey. The act of reflecting on a speech, evaluating its success, and understanding how the Moment was created or missed is crucial for growth. This process allows speakers to learn from both triumphs and failures.

Historical and Recent Anecdote

1. **Historical Anecdote:** After his "Gettysburg Address," President Lincoln felt he had failed to connect with the audience. However, the reflection and evaluation of others turned it into an iconic piece of oratory.

2. **Recent Anecdote:** Many modern speakers actively seek feedback through social media, engaging directly with their audience to understand what resonated and what didn't.

Relating it to the Speaker's Canvas

Reflection, evaluation, and feedback align with Monitoring, Moment, and Members in the 7 Ms Speaker's Canvas. Understanding how you've connected with the audience and what moments made an impact ensures that future speeches will be even more effective.

Details Discussing Key Advice

1. **Seek Honest Feedback:** Encourage audience members or colleagues to provide constructive criticism.

2. **Analyze Your Performance:** Review recordings of your speech to identify areas for improvement.

3. **Recognize and Embrace Both Success and Failure:** Both are valuable teachers in the journey to master public speaking.

Anecdotes

1. **Contemporary Anecdote:** Oprah Winfrey often speaks about the importance of feedback and self-reflection in her speaking career. This continual process of growth has made her one of the most compelling speakers of our time.

2. **Historical Anecdotes:** Ancient Greek orators like Demosthenes would practice in front of mirrors and small, critical audiences to perfect their craft, reflecting on every gesture and tone.

Practical Advice

1. **Create a Feedback Loop:** Regularly engage with your audience or mentors to understand your impact.

2. **Set Clear Goals and Assess Them:** Know what you want to achieve with your speech and evaluate how well you met those objectives.

3. **Embrace a Growth Mindset:** Recognize that every speaking opportunity is a chance to learn and grow.

Conclusion

Understanding the Moment through reflection, evaluation, and feedback is a path to continuous improvement in public speaking. It deepens the connection with your audience, sharpens your skills, and enriches your future speeches.

Reflection and evaluation are the invisible threads that weave success into the fabric of public speaking. From Lincoln's self-doubt to Oprah's growth, understanding the Moment through feedback has shaped some of the most influential voices in history.

Chapter 5: The Medium

Introduction: Why Choosing the Right Medium is Essential

The medium is the bridge between the speaker and the audience. It's not just what you say, but how you say it. The right medium can make your message resonate with an audience; the wrong one can disconnect it. In the world of public speaking, the medium you choose could be the difference between a standing ovation and a silent room.

Why this M is Important

Think of the medium as a vehicle. You wouldn't drive a sports car through a muddy field, nor would you take a tractor on a high-speed chase. Each has its place, and so does the medium in the context of your message.

Historical and Recent Anecdote

Historically, Winston Churchill's wartime speeches were delivered through the radio. The crackling voice, full of determination, reached homes and instilled hope and courage. In contrast, in recent times, TED Talks have made use of visual presentations, supporting words with images and graphics, and brought complex ideas to life.

Relating it to the Speaker's Canvas

The medium is like the texture of a painting in the speaker's canvas. It provides the feel, the connection, and sets the tone. Selecting the right medium is about understanding your audience, your message, and the context in which you're speaking.

Details Discussing Key Advice

1. **Know Your Audience:** If your audience is tech-savvy, a digital presentation might work; if not, a simpler approach could be more effective.

2. **Match the Message:** The medium should align with the content. A heartfelt story might best be told without any distractions, while a business proposal might require graphs and charts.

3. **Consider the Environment:** A large conference hall may require different tools than a small classroom.

Three Anecdotes

1. **Contemporary:** Elon Musk's presentation about SpaceX's plans for Mars was filled with 3D models and simulations. It made the futuristic concept feel tangible.

2. **Historical:** Martin Luther King, Jr.'s "I Have a Dream" speech didn't need visual aids; his voice and words were enough to paint a picture.

3. **Historical:** Steve Jobs's iPhone launch presentation in 2007, where he masterfully used slides and a live demonstration, set a new standard for product unveiling.

Practical Advice

Know your audience, your message, and your environment, and choose the medium that best aligns with these three. Test and rehearse to ensure everything flows smoothly.

Conclusion

Choosing the right medium is an art and a science. It requires thoughtfulness and intention. It's not just about what feels right to you, but what will resonate with your audience. The right medium can elevate your speech from ordinary to extraordinary.

Bibliography

- "Winston Churchill: The Wilderness Years 1928-39," Martin Gilbert, 1981.
- "Talk Like TED: The 9 Public-Speaking Secrets of the World's Top Minds," Carmine Gallo, 2014.
- "Steve Jobs," Walter Isaacson, 2011.

Recommended Reading

- "Resonate: Present Visual Stories that Transform Audiences," Nancy Duarte, 2010.
- "The Presentation Secrets of Steve Jobs," Carmine Gallo, 2009.

Technology & Innovation: Leveraging Tools and Platforms

In the modern age, the tools we have at our disposal are ever-changing and evolving. As a speaker, the technological medium you choose can make your message more dynamic, engaging, and accessible. This section will explore how technology and innovation play vital roles in the medium of public speaking.

Why this Aspect of the Medium is Important

Technology isn't just a fancy addition to a speech; it can be a transformative tool. From PowerPoint slides to augmented reality experiences, leveraging technology can make complex ideas more digestible and create a memorable experience for the audience.

Historical and Recent Anecdote

Historical: In the 1960s, John F. Kennedy utilized live television broadcasts to communicate with the nation. This medium allowed him to reach millions of homes, making the presidency more accessible to the common citizen.

Recent: Tony Robbins, a motivational speaker, employs immersive 360-degree videos and virtual reality in his seminars to create an engaging, interactive experience that connects with a global audience.

Relating it to the Speaker's Canvas

Just as a painter uses various brushes and techniques to create texture and depth, a speaker can employ technology to add layers to their presentation. It can enhance the visual and auditory aspects, creating a more holistic experience.

Details Discussing Key Advice

1. **Understand Your Tools:** Whether it's a simple projector or virtual reality headset, knowing how to use technology is essential.

2. **Align with Your Message:** Technology should amplify your message, not overshadow it. Use it to reinforce your points.

3. **Consider Accessibility:** Ensure that everyone in your audience can experience the technology, regardless of their familiarity with it.

Three Anecdotes

1. **Contemporary:** Brene Brown's use of simple yet effective visuals in her TED Talk about vulnerability made a complex subject more approachable.

2. **Historical:** The televised Nixon-Kennedy debate in 1960 showed how the medium of television could influence perception. Nixon appeared less comfortable on TV, affecting viewers' opinions.

3. **Historical:** Alan Turing's use of technology to explain computational concepts in his lectures paved the way for modern computer science education.

Practical Advice

Don't shy away from exploring new tools and platforms, but always keep the focus on your message. Practice with technology beforehand, and ensure it complements rather than competes with your content.

Conclusion

Technology and innovation in public speaking are not about using the latest gadgets for the sake of it. They're about enhancing the connection between the speaker and the audience, making the message more relatable and engaging. Like a skilled artist, use technology to paint a vivid picture without losing the essence of your message.

Bibliography

- "The Kennedy Mystique: Creating Camelot," Jon Goodman, 2006.
- "Talk Like TED: The 9 Public-Speaking Secrets of the World's Top Minds," Carmine Gallo, 2014.
- "Alan Turing: The Enigma," Andrew Hodges, 1983.

Recommended Reading

- "Illuminate: Ignite Change Through Speeches, Stories, Ceremonies, and Symbols," Nancy Duarte & Patti Sanchez, 2016.
- "TED Talks: The Official TED Guide to Public Speaking," Chris Anderson, 2016.

Anecdotes: Historical and Recent Examples of Medium Usage

Anecdotes are the heartbeat of a speech. They breathe life into facts and figures, making them memorable and relatable. This section will explore how different mediums have been employed throughout history and in recent times to share anecdotes that connect, inspire, and educate.

Why this Aspect of the Medium is Important

Anecdotes make messages come alive. The medium through which they are conveyed can enhance or detract from their impact. Choosing the right medium to share anecdotes ensures that they resonate with the audience and reinforce the speaker's message.

Historical and Recent Anecdote

Historical: Mark Twain was renowned for his storytelling, using his charismatic voice and body language as mediums to bring his tales to life in public lectures.

Recent: Chimamanda Ngozi Adichie's TED Talk "The Danger of a Single Story" masterfully blends her eloquent speech with video clips to emphasize her point about cultural misunderstanding.

Relating it to the Speaker's Canvas

The medium used to convey anecdotes is the color palette in the speaker's canvas. It sets the tone, emotion, and vibrancy of the story. A well-chosen medium makes an anecdote more vivid and impactful.

Details Discussing Key Advice

1. **Match the Medium to the Mood:** A humorous story may benefit from a lively video clip, while a somber tale may be best delivered through the raw power of speech alone.
2. **Keep It Authentic:** Ensure that the medium doesn't overshadow the authenticity of the anecdote.
3. **Test the Impact:** Try different mediums with a sample audience to see what resonates best.

Three Anecdotes

1. **Contemporary:** Malala Yousafzai's use of personal photos during speeches about education and women's rights creates a profound connection between her life story and her advocacy.
2. **Historical:** During his "Gettysburg Address," Abraham Lincoln's powerful oration alone served as the medium, needing no visual aids to etch his words into the annals of history.
3. **Historical:** Oprah Winfrey's use of live interviews in her talk show made personal stories feel immediate and relatable to viewers around the world.

Practical Advice

Consider the emotional tone, audience's familiarity, and context when selecting the medium for anecdotes. Sometimes, simplicity is powerful; other times, a visual or auditory aid can add depth.

Conclusion

Anecdotes bridge the gap between speaker and audience, turning abstract ideas into relatable stories. The medium through which they're conveyed can make them memorable or forgettable. Like choosing the right brush for a painting, selecting the appropriate medium for anecdotes requires insight, sensitivity, and an understanding of the audience.

Bibliography

- "Mark Twain: A Biography," Albert Bigelow Paine, 1912.
- "The Oprah Winfrey Show: Reflections on an American Legacy," Deborah Davis, 2011.
- "I Am Malala: The Girl Who Stood Up for Education and Was Shot by the Taliban," Malala Yousafzai, 2013.

Recommended Reading

- "Made to Stick: Why Some Ideas Survive and Others Die," Chip and Dan Heath, 2007.
- "Storytelling with Data: A Data Visualization Guide for Business Professionals," Cole Nussbaumer Knaflic, 2015.

Storytelling & Narrative Structure: Medium as a Storytelling Tool

The narrative structure of a speech is like the plot of a novel. It guides the audience along a journey, keeping them engaged and invested. The medium through which this narrative is conveyed can enhance or undermine the storytelling. Let's explore how to leverage medium as a storytelling tool.

Why this Aspect of the Medium is Important

The medium adds depth to the narrative, creating a sensory experience that draws the audience into the story. Whether it's a gripping audio clip or an evocative image, the right medium can make a story more vivid and engaging.

Historical and Recent Anecdote

Historical: The Fireside Chats by President Franklin D. Roosevelt used radio as a medium to narrate the nation's progress during the Great Depression, creating a sense of intimacy and trust.

Recent: Sir Ken Robinson's TED Talk on education used humor, casual tone, and simple visuals to create a compelling narrative about the need for creativity in schools.

Relating it to the Speaker's Canvas

In the speaker's canvas, the medium of storytelling is like the perspective in a painting. It determines how the audience sees and experiences the story, guiding their emotions and understanding.

Details Discussing Key Advice

1. **Create a Flow:** The medium must support the narrative flow, keeping the audience engaged without jarring interruptions.

2. **Enhance, Don't Distract:** Choose a medium that amplifies the story without drawing attention away from it.

3. **Consider the Emotional Impact:** A powerful image or haunting melody can evoke emotions that words alone might not.

Three Anecdotes

1. **Contemporary:** J.K. Rowling's Harvard commencement speech, intertwined with her personal story and minimal visuals, inspired graduates to embrace failure as a means to success.

2. **Historical:** Charlie Chaplin's speech in "The Great Dictator" used film as a medium to create a powerful narrative against tyranny, with visuals and sound enhancing his message.

3. **Historical:** William Jennings Bryan's "Cross of Gold" speech used vivid imagery and rhetorical flourish without any visual aids, captivating his audience through sheer oratory.

Practical Advice

The medium must serve the story. Test various mediums to see which best conveys the narrative's tone, pace, and emotional impact. Less can be more if it supports the storytelling.

Conclusion

The medium in storytelling is like the director in a film, guiding the audience's experience and shaping their perception. Whether it's through words, images, or sounds, the medium chosen must align with the narrative's essence, adding depth without overshadowing the story itself.

Bibliography

- "FDR's Fireside Chats," Russell D. Buhite, 1992.
- "The Element: How Finding Your Passion Changes Everything," Sir Ken Robinson, 2009.
- "Charlie Chaplin: A Brief Life," Peter Ackroyd, 2014.

Recommended Reading

- "The Art of Storytelling: Easy Steps to Presenting an Unforgettable Story," John Walsh, 2013.
- "Resonate: Present Visual Stories that Transform Audiences," Nancy Duarte, 2010.

Speaker's Canvas Relation: Medium's Role in Effective Speaking

In the world of public speaking, the Speaker's Canvas is a conceptual framework that helps orchestrate the elements of a speech, akin to how an artist arranges elements on a canvas. The medium is an integral part of this canvas, influencing how the message is perceived and resonated.

This section explores the role of medium within the Speaker's Canvas.

Why this Aspect of the Medium is Important

The medium serves as a conduit between the speaker's intent and the audience's understanding. It influences how the message is received, its emotional impact, and the engagement level of the audience. Understanding the medium's role in the Speaker's Canvas is crucial for effective speaking.

Historical and Recent Anecdote

Historical: Winston Churchill's inspiring speeches during WWII were delivered through radio broadcasts, a medium that reached the masses and fueled a sense of unity.

Recent: Sheryl Sandberg's Lean In presentations often employ a blend of personal stories and data-driven slides, using the medium to strengthen her advocacy for women's empowerment.

Relating it to the Speaker's Canvas

In the Speaker's Canvas, the medium functions like the texture on a painting. It adds depth and nuance, helping to convey the speaker's voice, tone, and emotion. Whether using visuals, sound, or interactive elements, the medium must align with the overall composition of the speech.

Details Discussing Key Advice

1. **Harmonize with Other Elements:** The medium must blend with the message, messenger, moment,

and other aspects of the Speaker's Canvas to create a cohesive experience.

2. **Select Wisely:** A mismatched medium can distort the message. Choose one that fits the audience, content, and context.

3. **Innovate Thoughtfully:** Explore new mediums but ensure they enhance, not complicate, the speech.

Three Anecdotes

1. **Contemporary:** Elon Musk's product launch events often use live demonstrations and multimedia presentations, aligning the medium with his innovative brand image.

2. **Historical:** Dr. Martin Luther King Jr.'s "I Have a Dream" speech relied on the power of oration, using voice modulation and body language as the medium to convey a stirring message.

3. **Historical:** Susan B. Anthony's speeches on women's suffrage were often accompanied by pamphlets and printed materials, a medium that reinforced her message in a pre-electronic era.

Practical Advice

Aligning the medium with other elements of the Speaker's Canvas ensures that it serves the message without overwhelming it. Consistency and thoughtful innovation are key to using the medium effectively.

Conclusion

The medium is more than just a delivery mechanism; it's a vital part of the artistic composition of a speech. Just as an artist selects the right texture for a painting, a speaker must choose the medium that complements and enhances the message, fitting seamlessly into the Speaker's Canvas.

Bibliography

- "Churchill: The Power of Words," Winston Churchill, 2012.
- "Lean In: Women, Work, and the Will to Lead," Sheryl Sandberg, 2013.
- "Susan B. Anthony: A Biography," Kathleen Barry, 1988.

Recommended Reading

- "The Medium is the Massage," Marshall McLuhan and Quentin Fiore, 1967.
- "Slide:ology: The Art and Science of Creating Great Presentations," Nancy Duarte, 2008.

Adaptation & Flexibility: Changing Mediums as Needed

Public speaking is a dynamic practice that often requires agility and responsiveness. As with the brush strokes of an artist who adjusts to the texture of the canvas, a speaker must adapt the medium to fit the audience, the environment, and even unexpected circumstances.

Why this Aspect of the Medium is Important

A rigid attachment to a specific medium can hinder a speech's impact. Flexibility allows a speaker to connect with the audience more effectively, tailoring the medium to the moment and making the message more resonant.

Historical and Recent Anecdote

Historical: When his PowerPoint failed, Steve Jobs seamlessly transitioned to an impromptu talk during the iPhone launch, demonstrating the importance of adaptability.

Recent: Greta Thunberg's speeches on climate change vary in medium, from addressing the UN to engaging with social media, adapting to reach different audiences globally.

Relating it to the Speaker's Canvas

In the Speaker's Canvas, adaptation and flexibility in the medium function as the shades and hues that add richness and dimension. Being able to modify the medium enhances the speaker's ability to create a more vivid and compelling picture.

Details Discussing Key Advice

1. **Anticipate and Prepare:** Have backup plans for potential issues, such as technology failures or changes in the audience's mood.

2. **Read the Audience:** Adjust the medium based on the audience's reactions and engagement.

3. **Stay True to the Message:** While adapting, ensure that the core message remains consistent and clear.

Three Anecdotes

1. **Contemporary:** Malala Yousafzai, in promoting education for girls, varies her medium from personal storytelling in speeches to documentaries, adapting to different platforms.

2. **Historical:** Abraham Lincoln's Gettysburg Address was notably brief, adapting to the somber mood and context, without visual or auditory aids.

3. **Historical:** The Scopes Trial of 1925 saw Clarence Darrow using a variety of mediums, including courtroom speeches and newspaper articles, to adapt his defense strategy.

Practical Advice

Embrace flexibility as a strength rather than a liability. Preparing for various scenarios and being willing to change course can make a speech more relatable and impactful.

Conclusion

Adaptation and flexibility in the medium are like the subtle adjustments an artist makes to capture the essence of a scene. Recognizing when and how to change mediums can bring the message to life, creating a more authentic and resonant connection with the audience.

Bibliography

- "Steve Jobs," Walter Isaacson, 2011.

- "No One Is Too Small to Make a Difference," Greta Thunberg, 2019.
- "The Great Trials of Clarence Darrow," Donald McRae, 2009.

Recommended Reading

- "Adapt: Why Success Always Starts with Failure," Tim Harford, 2011.
- "Talk Like TED: The 9 Public-Speaking Secrets of the World's Top Minds," Carmine Gallo, 2014.

Detailed Discussion: Key Considerations for Medium Selection

The choice of medium in public speaking isn't merely about picking between PowerPoint or a microphone. It's a complex decision that can shape the entire experience of the speech. This section offers an in-depth look at the key considerations to guide this choice.

Why this Aspect of the Medium is Important

Selecting the right medium is like choosing the right instruments in an orchestra; it sets the tone, rhythm, and harmony of the speech. A mismatched medium can create discord, while the right choice amplifies the message.

Historical and Recent Anecdote

Historical: Thomas Edison used the phonograph, a cutting-edge invention of his time, to share his ideas and inventions, aligning his medium with his innovative persona.

Recent: Tony Robbins often employs an interactive approach, involving audience participation, reinforcing his messages about personal growth and empowerment.

Relating it to the Speaker's Canvas

Within the Speaker's Canvas, medium selection is akin to choosing the right colors and shades. It's not just about aesthetics but how those choices affect the overall perception of the artwork.

Details Discussing Key Advice

1. **Understand Your Audience:** Age, background, and expectations can significantly influence how a medium resonates.

2. **Align with the Message:** The medium must reflect and enhance the core message, not detract from it.

3. **Consider the Venue:** A large auditorium may require different mediums compared to an intimate conference room.

4. **Balance Innovation and Familiarity:** While new mediums can engage, they shouldn't confuse or alienate the audience.

Three Anecdotes

1. **Contemporary:** Michelle Obama's use of personal photographs in her book talks, aligning the visual medium with her intimate narratives.

2. **Historical:** Mahatma Gandhi's adoption of simple speech and handwritten letters to communicate his messages of non-violence and simplicity.
3. **Historical:** Franklin D. Roosevelt's use of radio for his Fireside Chats, selecting a medium that reflected the intimate and reassuring tone he wished to convey.

Practical Advice

A strategic approach to medium selection involves a nuanced understanding of the audience, context, and message. Practicing with different mediums and seeking feedback can lead to a more informed choice.

Conclusion

Selecting the right medium for a speech is a multifaceted decision that demands careful consideration. Like a master painter choosing the perfect shade, a speaker must select a medium that enhances the message, resonates with the audience, and fits the context.

Bibliography

- "Edison: A Biography," Matthew Josephson, 1959.
- "Awaken the Giant Within," Tony Robbins, 1991.
- "Becoming," Michelle Obama, 2018.

Recommended Reading

- "Presentation Zen: Simple Ideas on Presentation Design and Delivery," Garr Reynolds, 2011.

- "The Art of Public Speaking," Stephen Lucas, 2014.

Cultural Sensitivity & Global Perspective: Global Reach of Mediums

In an increasingly interconnected world, public speaking often transcends geographical and cultural boundaries. The choice of medium must be attuned not only to the local audience but also to a broader, more diverse global audience. This section explores the complexities of this crucial consideration.

Why this Aspect of the Medium is Important

Choosing a medium that acknowledges and respects cultural differences and global perspectives amplifies the power of a message. It ensures that the speech resonates across various cultural contexts, making it inclusive and accessible.

Historical and Recent Anecdote

Historical: In the early 20th century, Charlie Chaplin used silent films, a universal medium, to communicate across language barriers.

Recent: Malala Yousafzai's speech to the United Nations was broadcasted globally, choosing a medium that transcended national and cultural lines.

Relating it to the Speaker's Canvas

In the Speaker's Canvas, this aspect functions like the intricate patterns that connect different parts of a painting. It's about weaving a common thread through diverse elements, creating a harmonious and cohesive piece.

Details Discussing Key Advice

1. **Recognize Diversity:** Acknowledge the wide range of cultural norms and expectations that might influence how a medium is perceived.

2. **Adopt Universal Themes:** When speaking to a global audience, choose mediums that convey universal messages.

3. **Avoid Stereotypes:** Be cautious of using mediums that might unintentionally reinforce stereotypes or biases.

4. **Engage with Empathy:** Understand and respect different cultural values and perspectives, allowing the medium to build bridges rather than barriers.

Three Anecdotes

1. **Contemporary:** TED Talks use a standardized format that transcends cultural differences, using visuals and speech to connect with a global audience.

2. **Historical:** Nelson Mandela's speeches were often translated into various languages and distributed through multiple channels, ensuring accessibility.

3. **Historical:** During his travels, Marco Polo used storytelling and illustrations, mediums that allowed

him to share his experiences across different cultures.

Practical Advice

Global considerations in medium selection require an open mind, empathy, and awareness. Collaborating with cultural experts and being open to feedback can foster sensitivity and inclusiveness.

Conclusion

The global reach of mediums is akin to the universal language of art. A mindful and empathetic approach to medium selection can create a speech that speaks across cultures and resonates with a diverse audience, painting a picture that's both rich and inclusive.

Bibliography

- "Charlie Chaplin: A Brief Life," Peter Ackroyd, 2014.
- "I Am Malala: The Girl Who Stood Up for Education and Was Shot by the Taliban," Malala Yousafzai, 2013.
- "The Travels of Marco Polo," Marco Polo, 1958.

Recommended Reading

- "The Culture Map: Breaking Through the Invisible Boundaries of Global Business," Erin Meyer, 2014.
- "Speak Up, Show Up, and Stand Out: The 9 Communication Rules You Need to Succeed," Loretta Malandro, 2014.

Practical Advice: Enhancing Medium Utilization

Once the medium is selected, how do you make the most of it? This section dives into the nitty-gritty of using a medium to its fullest potential, providing actionable insights and tips.

Why this Aspect of the Medium is Important

Mastering the chosen medium can elevate a speech from mundane to extraordinary. It's akin to a musician who not only selects the right instrument but plays it with virtuosity.

Historical and Recent Anecdote

Historical: Winston Churchill's mastery of radio during WWII helped him rally the British nation, turning a medium into a tool of resilience.

Recent: Oprah Winfrey's use of multimedia in her talks allows her to create an engaging experience that transcends mere words, turning speeches into impactful experiences.

Relating it to the Speaker's Canvas

This aspect is the final brushstroke that brings the painting to life in the Speaker's Canvas. It's about finessing and enhancing, turning a choice of medium into an art form.

Details Discussing Key Advice

1. **Master the Tools:** Whether it's a microphone or a digital platform, understanding the technical aspects ensures smooth delivery.

2. **Create Engagement:** Utilize the medium to connect, engage, and involve the audience.

3. **Emphasize Aesthetics:** Visual or auditory aesthetics in your medium can make a significant impact.

4. **Practice Makes Perfect:** Rehearsing with the chosen medium will help you become more comfortable and effective.

Three Anecdotes

1. **Contemporary:** Steve Jobs' presentation style, filled with sleek slides and minimal text, became a hallmark of Apple's product launches, showing mastery over the visual medium.

2. **Historical:** Martin Luther King Jr.'s ability to use vocal modulation and body language turned his speeches into legendary performances.

3. **Historical:** Florence Nightingale used graphs and charts, an unusual medium at her time, to present her findings about sanitation in hospitals effectively.

Practical Advice

Invest time in understanding and practicing with the chosen medium. Consider taking workshops or seeking professional guidance if needed. Like any skill, mastery comes with dedication and effort.

Conclusion

Enhancing medium utilization is about turning a tool into an extension of yourself as a speaker. It's the flourish that makes the message resonate more powerfully, creating a memorable experience for the audience.

Bibliography

- "Churchill: A Life," Martin Gilbert, 1991.
- "What I Know for Sure," Oprah Winfrey, 2014.
- "Steve Jobs: A Biography," Walter Isaacson, 2011.

Recommended Reading

- "Slide:ology: The Art and Science of Creating Great Presentations," Nancy Duarte, 2008.
- "Voice Training: Get A Better Voice And Improve Your Voice With Voice Exercises," Michael Lawrence, 2019.

Conclusion: Evaluation & Feedback on Medium Selection

Selecting and utilizing the right medium in public speaking is a nuanced and multifaceted task. This concluding section synthesizes the key insights, reflecting on the importance of thoughtful evaluation and continual feedback.

Why the Medium's Evaluation and Feedback are Important

Medium selection isn't a one-time decision; it's a continual process that benefits from constant evaluation and feedback. It ensures that the choice remains aligned with the ever-evolving audience, context, and message.

Historical and Recent Anecdote

Historical: Abraham Lincoln continually refined his speeches, adapting his medium according to audience feedback, as evidenced in his different versions of the Gettysburg Address.

Recent: TED Conferences continually innovate and adapt their presentation formats based on audience feedback, keeping their global platform fresh and engaging.

Relating it to the Speaker's Canvas

In the Speaker's Canvas, evaluation and feedback are like the careful examination of the painting from various angles, adjusting and refining to create the desired effect.

Details Discussing Key Advice

1. **Solicit Feedback:** Encourage audience feedback on how the medium enhanced or hindered the experience.
2. **Self-Evaluate:** Review recordings, assess your comfort level, and identify areas for improvement.

3. **Adapt and Innovate:** Don't be afraid to change the medium if it's not resonating. Flexibility can lead to growth.
4. **Consider Expert Review:** Sometimes, a professional eye can offer invaluable insights.

Three Anecdotes

1. **Contemporary:** Elon Musk constantly tweaks his presentation style, from technical briefings to more audience-friendly reveals, reflecting his evolution as a speaker.
2. **Historical:** FDR's Fireside Chats were adjusted based on public response, leading to one of the most successful radio series in history.
3. **Historical:** Socrates' method of dialogue and questioning evolved through constant interaction and feedback with his audience.

Practical Advice

Keep an open mind, welcome critique, and be prepared to evolve. Evaluation and feedback are not about finding flaws but about continuous growth and alignment with the message and audience.

Conclusion

The journey through medium selection in public speaking is akin to an artist continually refining their masterpiece. Evaluation and feedback are the guiding lights that ensure the medium remains an effective and resonant tool. They remind us that public speaking is a living art form, always in dialogue with its audience.

Bibliography

- "Lincoln at Gettysburg: The Words That Remade America," Garry Wills, 1992.
- "TED Talks: The Official TED Guide to Public Speaking," Chris Anderson, 2016.
- "Socrates: A Man for Our Times," Paul Johnson, 2011.

Recommended Reading

- "Thanks for the Feedback: The Science and Art of Receiving Feedback Well," Douglas Stone and Sheila Heen, 2014.
- "The Presentation Secrets of Steve Jobs: How to Be Insanely Great in Front of Any Audience," Carmine Gallo, 2009.

Chapter 6: Monitoring

Why Monitoring is Important

In the world of public speaking, monitoring is not just a simple act of observation; it's the lifeline that connects the speaker to the audience. It's an intuitive dance, a delicate give-and-take that keeps a speech lively and relevant.

Historical and Recent Anecdote Why Monitoring is Important

- **Historical Anecdote**: Winston Churchill was known for his powerful speeches during World War II. But what made him remarkable was his ability to monitor his audience, adjusting his tone and content according to their reactions. During his "We Shall Fight on the Beaches" speech, he noticed a shift in the crowd's energy, subtly modifying his delivery to re-engage them, turning what could have been a monotonous recital into a rallying cry.

- **Recent Anecdote**: In the age of TED Talks and live-streaming, monitoring has taken on new dimensions. Monica Lewinsky's TED Talk on the price of shame is a notable example. By monitoring the room's temperature, she was able to navigate a sensitive subject with grace, adjusting her pace, and emphasis in real-time to maintain connection with her audience.

Relating it to the Speaker's Canvas

Monitoring is a crucial component of the 7 Ms speaker's canvas. It transcends the boundaries of mere observation and turns speaking into a dynamic conversation. It's not just about talking; it's about listening, observing, and responding. The ability to perceive and adapt to the audience's needs and reactions is essential for a speech's success.

Details Discussing Key Advice or Considerations for Improving Monitoring

1. **Observe Body Language**: Watch for signs of engagement or disinterest.

2. **Listen to Audience Reactions**: Applause, laughter, or silence can speak volumes.

3. **Ask for Feedback**: Sometimes, direct questions can help gauge the audience's interest and understanding.

Anecdotes

- **Contemporary**: Michelle Obama's ability to connect with various audiences during her book tours shows excellent monitoring skills. Her empathetic approach, watching faces, and modifying her message allowed her to resonate with people from different backgrounds.

- **Historical Figures**:
    - **Martin Luther King Jr.**: His "I Have a Dream" speech was not just a prepared text; it was a live dialogue with his audience. He

sensed the crowd's energy and adjusted his speech to elevate it into an iconic moment in history.

- **Abraham Lincoln**: During the Lincoln-Douglas debates, Lincoln's ability to monitor the crowd and opponents allowed him to tailor his arguments, engaging listeners with a blend of logic and emotion.

Practical Advice How the User Can Improve Their Speech Using Monitoring

1. **Build Awareness**: Start by recognizing your audience's needs and expectations.
2. **Adapt in Real Time**: Don't be afraid to stray from your script if you feel the audience needs something different.
3. **Use Technology**: Tools like live-polls and audience response systems can provide real-time insights.

Conclusion

Monitoring is more than a skill; it's an art. It represents a symbiotic relationship between the speaker and the audience, turning a speech into a shared experience. Embracing monitoring can turn an ordinary speech into an extraordinary connection.

Bibliography

1. Churchill, Winston. "We Shall Fight on the Beaches." House of Commons, 4 June 1940.

2. Lewinsky, Monica. "The Price of Shame." TED, March 2015.

3. Obama, Michelle. "Becoming: An Intimate Conversation with Michelle Obama." Live Nation, 2018-2019.

Recommended Reading

1. "The Art of Public Speaking" by Dale Carnegie

2. "Talk Like TED: The 9 Public Speaking Secrets of the World's Top Minds" by Carmine Gallo

3. "Steal the Show: From Speeches to Job Interviews to Deal-Closing Pitches" by Michael Port

Emotional Intelligence & Connection: Understanding Reactions

Why Emotional Intelligence is Important in Monitoring

Emotional intelligence is the ability to recognize and understand emotions in oneself and others, and the ability to use this awareness to manage behavior and relationships. In the context of public speaking, it's a vital tool for monitoring. Being able to read the room and connect with the audience's emotions can transform a speech from a monologue into a dialogue.

Historical and Recent Anecdote Why Emotional Intelligence is Important

- **Historical Anecdote**: Franklin D. Roosevelt's "Fireside Chats" were revolutionary not just for the medium (radio) but for the empathetic connection he forged with the American people. He could sense their fears during the Great Depression and World War II, responding with a calm and reassuring tone that felt both presidential and paternal.

- **Recent Anecdote**: Oprah Winfrey's 2018 speech at the Golden Globes demonstrated her acute emotional intelligence. Her understanding of the audience's feelings and the cultural moment allowed her to deliver a speech that was both personally moving and universally resonant.

Relating it to the Speaker's Canvas

Within the framework of the 7 Ms, emotional intelligence aligns with "Monitoring," enriching the speaker's ability to connect on a deeper level. It's not enough to recognize whether the audience is engaged or bored; a speaker must understand why. Emotional intelligence provides that why, allowing for more nuanced and effective communication.

Details Discussing Key Advice or Considerations for Improving Emotional Intelligence

1. **Develop Self-Awareness**: Recognize your emotions and how they might affect your performance.

2. **Build Empathy**: Try to understand the feelings of the audience and respond to them.

3. **Manage Emotions**: Use emotional information to adapt your speech and create a meaningful connection.

Anecdotes

- **Contemporary**: Brene Brown's research and talks on vulnerability show how emotional intelligence can foster deeper connections. Her ability to share personal stories and resonate with the audience's emotions makes her a standout speaker.

- **Historical Figures**:
    - **Mahatma Gandhi**: His ability to connect with people's hopes and fears played a crucial role in India's independence movement. Gandhi's emotional intelligence made him not just a leader but a symbol of hope.
    - **Nelson Mandela**: In post-apartheid South Africa, Mandela's emotional intelligence helped heal a divided nation. He understood the pain, anger, and hope of his people and spoke in a way that united them.

Practical Advice How the User Can Improve Their Speech Using Emotional Intelligence

1. **Learn to Listen**: Not just with your ears, but with your heart. Pay attention to what's unsaid.

2. **Reflect and Adapt**: Use the emotional cues from the audience to tailor your message.

3. **Practice Empathy**: Put yourself in the audience's shoes and speak to their needs and desires.

Conclusion

Emotional intelligence is not just a buzzword; it's a crucial component of effective monitoring in public speaking. It takes the speaker beyond the surface, into a realm of deeper understanding and connection. Whether addressing a small group or speaking to millions, cultivating emotional intelligence can transform a speaker's ability to resonate and inspire.

Bibliography

1. Roosevelt, Franklin D. "The Fireside Chats." 1933-1944.

2. Winfrey, Oprah. "Golden Globes Speech." 2018.

3. Brown, Brene. "The Power of Vulnerability." TEDxHouston, 2010.

Recommended Reading

1. "Emotional Intelligence 2.0" by Travis Bradberry and Jean Greaves

2. "Dare to Lead: Brave Work. Tough Conversations. Whole Hearts." by Brene Brown

3. "Long Walk to Freedom: The Autobiography of Nelson Mandela" by Nelson Mandela

Anecdotes: Examples of Effective Monitoring

Why Anecdotes are Important

Anecdotes, those small stories or examples, bring a concept to life. They make abstract ideas tangible and relatable. In public speaking, effective anecdotes serve as snapshots, offering glimpses into the subject matter. Here we will explore how monitoring through insightful anecdotes can profoundly impact both the speaker and the audience.

Historical and Recent Anecdote Why Anecdotes are Important in Monitoring

- **Historical Anecdote**: Mark Twain was a master at weaving anecdotes into his speeches. His humorous and poignant stories weren't just entertaining; they were a tool to monitor his audience. By observing their reactions to different anecdotes, he could adjust his speech, keeping them engaged and entertained.

- **Recent Anecdote**: Malala Yousafzai, the young advocate for girls' education, uses personal anecdotes to connect with audiences around the world. Her stories aren't merely illustrative; they're monitoring devices. She watches how people respond to her stories and adjusts her message to make sure it resonates with every listener.

Relating it to the Speaker's Canvas

In the 7 Ms framework, anecdotes align with "Monitoring" by giving speakers a direct insight into their audience's minds and hearts. They serve as mirrors, reflecting the audience's thoughts and feelings, allowing the speaker to adjust, clarify, or emphasize particular points.

Details Discussing Key Advice or Considerations for Improving the Use of Anecdotes

1. **Choose Relevant Anecdotes**: Your stories must relate to your main message.
2. **Observe the Reaction**: Watch how the audience responds and be ready to adjust.
3. **Balance Humor and Seriousness**: Anecdotes can be funny, inspiring, or sobering, but they should always serve your speech's overall purpose.

Anecdotes

- **Contemporary**: Steve Jobs' commencement address at Stanford in 2005 is filled with personal anecdotes that are both inspiring and monitoring tools. He watched how students reacted to his stories and used those cues to navigate his speech.
- **Historical Figures**:
    - **John F. Kennedy**: In his presidential campaign, Kennedy would often share anecdotes from his military service. These stories helped him monitor public sentiment

and adapt his message to connect with various audiences.

- **Sojourner Truth**: The famous "Ain't I a Woman?" speech is filled with personal anecdotes that Truth used to gauge her audience's attitudes toward gender and racial equality. Her ability to read and respond to the crowd's reactions made her a compelling orator.

Practical Advice How the User Can Improve Their Speech Using Anecdotes

1. **Craft Your Stories**: Prepare anecdotes that illustrate your key points, but be flexible enough to adjust them on the fly.

2. **Read the Room**: If an anecdote falls flat, don't dwell on it. Move on and use the feedback for your next point.

3. **Mix It Up**: Use different types of anecdotes to keep your audience engaged and provide a multi-dimensional perspective.

Conclusion

Anecdotes are not mere decorations in a speech; they are instrumental in monitoring and connecting with the audience. The most memorable speakers are often those who can tell a story that reaches out and touches listeners, guiding them along the intended path. The mastery of anecdotes adds a layer of richness to public speaking, creating a shared experience that goes beyond mere words.

Bibliography

1. Twain, Mark. "Speeches by Mark Twain." Harper & Brothers, 1910.

2. Yousafzai, Malala. "I Am Malala: The Girl Who Stood Up for Education and Was Shot by the Taliban." Little, Brown and Company, 2013.

3. Jobs, Steve. "Commencement Address at Stanford University." 2005.

Recommended Reading

1. "Made to Stick: Why Some Ideas Survive and Others Die" by Chip Heath and Dan Heath

2. "The Storyteller's Secret: From TED Speakers to Business Legends, Why Some Ideas Catch On and Others Don't" by Carmine Gallo

3. "Tell to Win: Connect, Persuade, and Triumph with the Hidden Power of Story" by Peter Guber

Rhetorical Techniques: Utilizing Persuasion in Monitoring

Why Rhetorical Techniques are Important in Monitoring

Rhetoric is the art of persuasive communication. Through the strategic use of rhetorical techniques, a speaker can monitor the audience's reactions, fine-tune their approach, and guide listeners toward a desired conclusion. Rhetoric isn't about manipulation; it's about understanding and aligning with the audience's needs, values, and emotions.

Historical and Recent Anecdote Why Rhetorical Techniques are Important

- **Historical Anecdote**: Winston Churchill's speeches during World War II were laden with rhetorical strategies. He used repetition, metaphors, and strong imagery to unite the British people. By monitoring their reaction, he knew when to push harder and when to offer comfort.

- **Recent Anecdote**: Former President Barack Obama's rhetorical skills are widely admired. His use of anaphora (repeating the beginning of successive sentences) and other techniques helped him monitor and engage with his audience, whether addressing the nation or speaking to small communities.

Relating it to the Speaker's Canvas

In the 7 Ms framework, rhetorical techniques fit into "Monitoring" by serving as a tool for gauging and influencing the audience's reaction. They allow speakers to communicate more dynamically and responsively, adapting their speech to the audience's needs and interests.

Details Discussing Key Advice or Considerations for Utilizing Rhetorical Techniques

1. **Know Your Audience**: Different techniques will resonate with different crowds, so choose wisely.

2. **Master the Tools**: Learn and practice rhetorical strategies such as ethos (credibility), pathos (emotion), and logos (logic).

3. **Balance is Key**: Overuse can lead to a lack of authenticity. Use rhetorical techniques to enhance, not overshadow, your message.

Anecdotes

- **Contemporary**: Dr. Martin Luther King Jr.'s "I Have a Dream" speech is a timeless example of rhetorical mastery. His repetition and metaphors still resonate today, showing how powerful these techniques can be in monitoring and moving an audience.

- **Historical Figures**:
  - **Julius Caesar**: Caesar's famous "Veni, Vidi, Vici" (I came, I saw, I conquered) showcases the power of brevity and parallelism.
  - **Susan B. Anthony**: Her speeches used rhetorical questions and appeals to morality to engage her audience in the fight for women's suffrage, continually adapting her message as she gauged their response.

Practical Advice How the User Can Improve Their Speech Using Rhetorical Techniques

1. **Study the Greats**: Learn from historical speeches that utilized rhetorical techniques effectively.

2. **Practice with Purpose**: Use these techniques in your daily communication to become more adept.

3. **Be Genuine**: Always ensure that the techniques you use align with your true message and values.

Conclusion

Utilizing rhetorical techniques is not just about sounding eloquent; it's a crucial aspect of monitoring the pulse of the audience and guiding them toward shared understanding. The ability to wield rhetoric with grace and intentionality separates good speakers from truly impactful ones.

Bibliography

1. Churchill, Winston. "Their Finest Hour." 1940.
2. Obama, Barack. "A More Perfect Union." 2008.
3. King, Martin Luther Jr. "I Have a Dream." 1963.

Recommended Reading

1. "Thank You for Arguing: What Aristotle, Lincoln, And Homer Simpson Can Teach Us About the Art of Persuasion" by Jay Heinrichs
2. "The Rhetoric of Rhetoric: The Quest for Effective Communication" by Wayne C. Booth
3. "Words Like Loaded Pistols: Rhetoric from Aristotle to Obama" by Sam Leith

Speaker's Canvas Relation: Monitoring in the Framework

Introduction: Importance of Monitoring within the Speaker's Canvas

Monitoring is not just an isolated skill; it's a thread that weaves through every aspect of the 7 Ms speaker's canvas. It touches Messenger, Message, Medium, Mobilization, Members, and Moment. Monitoring is the speaker's radar system, picking up feedback, gauging reactions, and adapting accordingly. Let's delve into how monitoring relates to the other aspects of the canvas and enhances the overall impact.

Historical and Recent Anecdote Why Monitoring is Important in the Speaker's Canvas

- **Historical Anecdote**: Theodore Roosevelt was a speaker who understood his audience. Whether addressing Congress or a crowd of workers, he knew how to monitor and adapt his language, tone, and content. His "Square Deal" speech was a classic example of connecting with his audience and adjusting his message to resonate with them.

- **Recent Anecdote**: Oprah Winfrey, a media mogul and renowned public speaker, continually monitors her audience, whether on television or a live stage. She connects, reassures, challenges, and inspires, always adapting to what she perceives in her listeners.

Relating Monitoring to Each Aspect of the Speaker's Canvas

1. **Messenger**: Monitoring helps the speaker align their persona with the audience's expectations and needs. It guides them to be authentic and relatable.

2. **Message**: By observing how the audience reacts to various parts of the speech, the speaker can emphasize what resonates and clarify what doesn't.

3. **Medium**: Choosing the right channel (speech, video, blog) requires monitoring the audience's preferences and comfort levels.

4. **Mobilization**: Gauging the audience's readiness to act helps the speaker mobilize them effectively towards a shared goal.

5. **Members**: Monitoring the diverse needs and reactions of the audience helps in customizing the speech to be inclusive and resonant.

6. **Moment**: Timing is everything. Monitoring guides when to inspire, when to challenge, when to console, aligning the speech with the unique moment.

Details Discussing Key Advice or Considerations for Improving Monitoring in the Speaker's Canvas

1. **Holistic Approach**: Don't isolate monitoring; integrate it into every aspect of your speaking strategy.

2. **Adaptive Flexibility**: Be ready to change course based on what you're sensing from the audience.
3. **Empathetic Connection**: Truly feel what your audience is experiencing, and let that guide your speech.

Anecdotes

- **Contemporary**: Tony Robbins, the motivational speaker, is known for his ability to read and adapt to his audience on the fly. His seminars are a living testament to how the 7 Ms canvas comes alive through constant monitoring.
- **Historical Figures**:
    - **Abraham Lincoln**: His Gettysburg Address was crafted with acute awareness of the nation's mood, reflecting his ability to monitor and connect with his audience's hearts.
    - **Eleanor Roosevelt**: A champion for human rights, she knew how to speak to different audiences, always monitoring and adjusting to create the strongest impact.

Practical Advice How the User Can Improve Their Speech Using Monitoring within the Speaker's Canvas

1. **Integrate Monitoring**: Make it a part of every stage of your speech preparation and delivery.
2. **Practice Empathy**: Put yourself in your audience's shoes to better understand and connect with them.

3. **Stay Open**: Be willing to adapt and grow through continuous monitoring and learning.

Conclusion

Monitoring is not merely a skill to be mastered in isolation; it's the glue that binds the speaker's canvas together. It brings responsiveness, resonance, and effectiveness into every speech, shaping the journey for both the speaker and the audience.

Bibliography

1. Roosevelt, Theodore. "The Square Deal." 1903.
2. Winfrey, Oprah. "Stanford Commencement Address." 2008.
3. Lincoln, Abraham. "The Gettysburg Address." 1863.

Recommended Reading

1. "The Charisma Myth: How Anyone Can Master the Art and Science of Personal Magnetism" by Olivia Fox Cabane
2. "Talk Like TED: The 9 Public-Speaking Secrets of the World's Top Minds" by Carmine Gallo
3. "Emotional Intelligence: Why It Can Matter More Than IQ" by Daniel Goleman

Technology & Innovation: Tools for Better Monitoring

Introduction: Importance of Technology and Innovation in Monitoring

In an age of digital advancement and innovation, technology provides speakers with powerful tools to monitor and engage with their audience. From social media analytics to audience response systems, technology offers real-time insights and interactivity that can make a speech more dynamic and responsive. Understanding these tools is not just a contemporary trend; it's a necessity in modern public speaking.

Historical and Recent Anecdote Why Technology and Innovation are Important

- **Historical Anecdote**: The use of teleprompters in the 1950s revolutionized public speaking by allowing speakers to maintain eye contact while following a script. Presidents like Dwight D. Eisenhower embraced this technology to enhance their connection with the audience.

- **Recent Anecdote**: TED Talks are a contemporary example of innovation in speaking. Using visual aids, interactive apps, and audience engagement tools, speakers at TED conferences create immersive experiences that captivate audiences worldwide.

Relating Technology and Innovation to the Speaker's Canvas

In the 7 Ms framework, technology acts as a support system for monitoring. It helps in gathering insights about the audience, enhancing the delivery of the message, and creating interactive experiences. Technology enables speakers to tune into the digital heartbeat of their audience and adapt accordingly.

Details Discussing Key Tools and Considerations for Improving Monitoring with Technology

1. **Social Media Analytics**: Understanding your audience through their digital footprints and online reactions.

2. **Audience Response Systems**: Tools like clickers or apps that allow real-time feedback during a speech.

3. **Virtual Reality**: Creating immersive speaking experiences to engage the audience in novel ways.

4. **Data Visualization**: Presenting complex information in accessible, visual formats.

Anecdotes

- **Contemporary**: Simon Sinek, known for his inspiring talks on leadership, leverages visual aids and technology to create engaging presentations that resonate with a wide audience.

- **Historical Figures**:
    - **Steve Jobs**: His product launches were masterclasses in using visual storytelling and sleek design to enhance a speech.

- **Margaret Thatcher**: The "Iron Lady" was known to use technology to her advantage, whether through her meticulous preparation using recorded speeches or her adaptation to television as a medium.

Practical Advice How the User Can Improve Their Speech Using Technology and Innovation

1. **Embrace Technology, Don't Fear It**: Get familiar with the latest tools that can enhance your connection with your audience.
2. **Balance Tech with Humanity**: Technology should enhance, not replace, the human connection in a speech.
3. **Stay Current**: The digital landscape is ever-changing. Keep up with the trends to remain relevant and effective.

Conclusion

Technology and innovation are powerful allies in the quest for effective public speaking. When used with care and intention, they can enhance the monitoring process, creating a speech that is not only informative but also engaging and responsive. They bridge the gap between the speaker and the audience in an increasingly interconnected world.

Bibliography

1. Eisenhower, Dwight D. "Farewell Address." 1961.
2. TED Conferences. Various Talks. 1984-present.

3. Jobs, Steve. "iPhone Launch." 2007.

Recommended Reading

1. "The Presentation Secrets of Steve Jobs: How to Be Insanely Great in Front of Any Audience" by Carmine Gallo

2. "Resonate: Present Visual Stories that Transform Audiences" by Nancy Duarte

3. "Digital Transformation: Survive and Thrive in an Era of Mass Extinction" by Thomas M. Siebel

Detailed Discussion: Improving Monitoring Skills

Introduction: The Art and Science of Monitoring

Improving monitoring skills isn't just about keeping an eye on the audience; it's about being attuned to the subtleties of human emotion, expression, and interaction. The detailed discussion that follows will provide insights into the various aspects of monitoring and guide you on a path to becoming a more responsive and empathetic speaker.

Historical and Recent Anecdote Why Improving Monitoring Skills is Essential

- **Historical Anecdote**: Winston Churchill, known for his powerful speeches during World War II, spent hours perfecting his delivery, understanding that monitoring the mood and reactions of his audience was paramount to galvanizing a nation.

- **Recent Anecdote**: Brene Brown, a renowned researcher and speaker on vulnerability, has mastered the art of reading her audience. Her talks resonate because she adapts to what she senses, whether speaking to corporate leaders or a room full of creatives.

Relating Improving Monitoring Skills to the Speaker's Canvas

Monitoring isn't merely an act; it's a skill that gets honed over time. It plays a pivotal role within the 7 Ms speaker's canvas, enabling the speaker to connect, adapt, and inspire. It cuts across Messenger, Message, Medium, Mobilization, Members, and Moment, reinforcing the interconnected nature of effective speaking.

Details Discussing Techniques and Considerations for Improving Monitoring Skills

1. **Observation**: Watch for body language, facial expressions, and eye contact. They speak volumes.

2. **Active Listening**: Engage with your audience's verbal feedback and adjust accordingly.

3. **Emotional Intelligence**: Develop the ability to read emotions and empathize with your audience.

4. **Feedback Loops**: Create opportunities for your audience to provide input during and after your speech.

5. **Adaptation**: Learn to change course when necessary, based on the real-time responses of your audience.

Anecdotes

- **Contemporary**: Sheryl Sandberg, Facebook COO and author of "Lean In," uses her understanding of her audience to make her speeches personal, relevant, and engaging.

- **Historical Figures**:
    - **Martin Luther King Jr.**: His "I Have a Dream" speech was a masterful display of empathy, understanding, and connection.
    - **Jane Goodall**: Her empathetic approach to speaking about conservation and primatology showcases how understanding and responding to an audience can turn a talk into a movement.

Practical Advice How the User Can Improve Their Speech Using Monitoring

1. **Learn to Read Non-Verbal Cues**: They often tell more than words.
2. **Engage Your Audience**: Ask questions, encourage participation, create a dialogue.
3. **Reflect and Adapt**: Post-speech, analyze what went well and what didn't, and adapt for future talks.

4. **Practice Makes Perfect**: Like any other skill, monitoring improves with practice.

Conclusion

Improving monitoring skills is akin to tuning an instrument. It's about finding the right balance, resonance, and rhythm with your audience. It's a continuous journey of learning, growing, and connecting. Monitoring transforms speaking from a monologue to a conversation, making it more authentic, relevant, and powerful.

Bibliography

1. Churchill, Winston. "Their Finest Hour." 1940.
2. Brown, Brene. "The Power of Vulnerability." TED Talk, 2010.
3. King, Martin Luther, Jr. "I Have a Dream." 1963.

Recommended Reading

1. "The Silent Language of Leaders: How Body Language Can Help—or Hurt—How You Lead" by Carol Kinsey Goman
2. "Just Listen: Discover the Secret to Getting Through to Absolutely Anyone" by Mark Goulston
3. "Emotional Intelligence 2.0" by Travis Bradberry and Jean Greaves

---

Evaluation & Feedback: Self-Evaluation and Audience Insights

Introduction: The Mirror of Evaluation and Feedback

Evaluation and feedback act as mirrors reflecting the effectiveness of a speech, both for the speaker and the audience. This two-way mirror enables a speaker to learn, grow, and refine their craft, transforming every speech into a stepping stone towards mastery.

Historical and Recent Anecdote Why Evaluation and Feedback are Crucial

- **Historical Anecdote**: Abraham Lincoln, after his famous Cooper Union speech, continually sought feedback from newspapers and colleagues. His self-evaluation and openness to criticism shaped his future speeches, including the Gettysburg Address.

- **Recent Anecdote**: Oprah Winfrey, a media mogul and master communicator, has embraced feedback throughout her career. Whether interviewing a guest or delivering an inspiring talk, she assesses her performance and seeks insights from her team.

Relating Evaluation and Feedback to the Speaker's Canvas

Evaluation and feedback interlace with every aspect of the 7 Ms canvas. They inform the Messenger, refine the Message, assess the Medium, guide Mobilization, and resonate with Members at the right Moment. It's a continuous loop that enriches the entire speaking experience.

Details Discussing Methods and Considerations for Evaluation and Feedback

1. **Self-Evaluation**: Reflecting on your performance, identifying strengths and areas for improvement.
2. **Peer Review**: Seeking honest feedback from colleagues or mentors.
3. **Audience Insights**: Utilizing surveys, Q&A sessions, and one-on-one interactions to gauge audience response.
4. **Professional Coaching**: Engaging with speaking experts to refine and enhance your skills.

Anecdotes

- **Contemporary**: Tony Robbins, a leading motivational speaker, has made it a practice to watch recordings of his speeches. He analyzes every detail, from body language to audience reaction.
- **Historical Figures**:
    - **John F. Kennedy**: Known for his eloquence, JFK worked closely with speechwriters and advisors, honing his skills through constant feedback.
    - **Maya Angelou**: Her growth as a poet and speaker was nurtured through self-reflection and feedback from mentors like James Baldwin.

Practical Advice How the User Can Improve Their Speech Through Evaluation and Feedback

1. **Embrace Feedback, Don't Shy Away**: See criticism as an opportunity to grow.

2. **Create a Feedback Loop**: Encourage audience participation and insights.

3. **Reflect and Act**: Take time to analyze your performance, and make necessary changes.

4. **Invest in Professional Guidance**: Sometimes an expert eye can see what you might miss.

Conclusion

Evaluation and feedback are the bedrock of continuous improvement in public speaking. They bridge the gap between perception and reality, giving speakers the tools to refine their craft, connect more deeply with their audience, and find their unique voice. It's a journey of self-discovery and growth, guided by reflection and insights from others.

Bibliography

1. Lincoln, Abraham. "Cooper Union Address." 1860.

2. Winfrey, Oprah. Various Interviews and Speeches. 1986-present.

3. Robbins, Tony. Various Seminars and Talks.

Recommended Reading

1. "Thanks for the Feedback: The Science and Art of Receiving Feedback Well" by Douglas Stone and Sheila Heen

2. "The Art of Possibility: Transforming Professional and Personal Life" by Rosamund Stone Zander and Benjamin Zander

3. "Speak with Impact: How to Command the Room and Influence Others" by Allison Shapira

Practical Advice: Tips for Better Monitoring

Introduction: Mastering the Art of Monitoring

Monitoring isn't merely about observing; it's about absorbing, interpreting, and responding. This section lays down practical advice to enhance your monitoring skills, turning a good speech into an outstanding one that resonates with every individual in the room.

Historical and Recent Anecdote Why Practical Advice for Better Monitoring is Essential

- **Historical Anecdote**: Theodore Roosevelt's "Man in the Arena" speech was not just a result of eloquent writing but also a masterful understanding of his audience. He monitored the crowd's reaction, pacing his delivery to amplify impact.

- **Recent Anecdote**: Simon Sinek, author of "Start with Why," emphasizes the importance of understanding your audience. His talks, brimming with passion, are shaped by his keen observation and responsiveness to the crowd's energy.

Relating Practical Advice for Better Monitoring to the Speaker's Canvas

The art of monitoring weaves through the 7 Ms, bridging Messenger, Message, Medium, Mobilization, Members, and Moment. It's the intuitive touch that adds life to a speech, making it more personal, vibrant, and engaging.

Details Discussing Practical Tips for Improving Monitoring Skills

1. **Know Your Audience**: Research who you are speaking to, their interests, needs, and expectations.

2. **Use Open Body Language**: Encourage interaction and feedback through your gestures and expressions.

3. **Invite Participation**: Foster a dialogue rather than a monologue.

4. **Utilize Technology**: Modern tools can help gauge audience engagement in real-time.

5. **Reflect and Adjust**: Be ready to pivot if something isn't resonating.

Anecdotes

- **Contemporary**: Malala Yousafzai, the youngest Nobel Prize laureate, expertly adjusts her tone and content based on her audience, whether addressing the United Nations or school children.

- **Historical Figures**:
    - **Steve Jobs**: His product launches were theatrical performances, timed and executed based on audience reactions.

- **Sojourner Truth**: Her famous "Ain't I a Woman?" speech showcased an intuitive understanding of the crowd and the moment.

Practical Advice How the User Can Improve Their Monitoring Skills

1. **Embrace Flexibility**: Stick to your script but be prepared to wander if the audience leads you.
2. **Invest in Training**: Workshops and seminars can sharpen your monitoring skills.
3. **Collaborate with Others**: Co-speakers and moderators can provide real-time insights.
4. **Trust Your Instincts**: Sometimes, your gut feeling is the best gauge of the audience's mood.

Conclusion

Better monitoring is about deepening the connection between speaker and listener. It's a dance where both lead and follow, creating a shared experience that transcends words. Practical insights shared here are not rules but tools, enhancing your ability to speak, listen, and engage in a way that leaves a lasting impact.

Bibliography

1. Roosevelt, Theodore. "Citizenship in a Republic." 1910.
2. Sinek, Simon. "How Great Leaders Inspire Action." TED Talk, 2009.
3. Jobs, Steve. Various Apple Keynotes.

Recommended Reading

1. "Presence: Bringing Your Boldest Self to Your Biggest Challenges" by Amy Cuddy
2. "Talk Like TED: The 9 Public-Speaking Secrets of the World's Top Minds" by Carmine Gallo
3. "The Charisma Myth: How Anyone Can Master the Art and Science of Personal Magnetism" by Olivia Fox Cabane

Conclusion: Reflecting on Monitoring Experiences

Introduction: The Symphonic Nature of Monitoring

Monitoring in public speaking is akin to conducting a symphony, with the speaker guiding the orchestra of listeners through a harmonious experience. This chapter's conclusion reflects on monitoring's pivotal role and offers a resounding affirmation of its essence in the art of speech.

Historical and Recent Anecdote: Why Monitoring is the Heartbeat of Speaking

- **Historical Anecdote**: Winston Churchill, a statesman and orator, crafted his speeches with meticulous precision. But what made them come alive was his ability to monitor the room and adapt, turning words into living history.
- **Recent Anecdote**: Brené Brown, known for her research on vulnerability, employs monitoring to

build trust and empathy with her audiences. Her talks are conversations rather than lectures, enabled by her attuned presence.

Relating Monitoring to the Speaker's Canvas

Monitoring is the thread that ties together all the 7 Ms, acting as both a guide and a gauge. It shapes the Messenger's authenticity, sharpens the Message's clarity, chooses the right Medium, fuels Mobilization, engages Members, and seizes the Moment. Monitoring is the heartbeat that gives life to every aspect of public speaking.

Reflections: The Art and Science of Monitoring

Monitoring is both art and science. It's a dance of intuition and intention, responsiveness and preparation. The best speakers:

1. **Listen as Much as They Speak**: They are tuned into the audience's needs and reactions.

2. **Adapt with Agility**: They pivot when needed, keeping the audience engaged.

3. **Use Technology Wisely**: Modern tools amplify their ability to connect.

4. **Embrace Feedback**: They grow through reflection and constructive criticism.

Anecdotes

- **Contemporary**: Michelle Obama, through her speaking engagements, exhibits a unique ability to connect and adapt, turning large venues into intimate conversations.

- **Historical Figures**:
    - **Martin Luther King Jr.**: His "I Have a Dream" speech was a masterful orchestration of words and pauses, shaped by the crowd's response.
    - **Margaret Thatcher**: The "Iron Lady" was known for her unwavering stance but also her ability to read and respond to her audience.

Concluding Thoughts

Monitoring is not merely a skill but a philosophy in the realm of public speaking. It transforms speeches from static monologues into dynamic dialogues, builds bridges of understanding, and fosters relationships that endure beyond the applause.

The journey through this chapter on Monitoring provides you, the reader, with insights, practical tips, historical lessons, and contemporary wisdom. It invites you to be more than a speaker; it beckons you to become a conductor of conversations, a master of moments, and a creator of connections.

Bibliography

1. Churchill, Winston. Various Speeches and Addresses.

2. Brown, Brené. "The Power of Vulnerability." TED Talk, 2010.

3. King, Martin Luther Jr. "I Have a Dream." 1963.

Recommended Reading

1. "Quiet: The Power of Introverts in a World That Can't Stop Talking" by Susan Cain

2. "The Art of Gathering: How We Meet and Why It Matters" by Priya Parker

3. "Made to Stick: Why Some Ideas Survive and Others Die" by Chip Heath and Dan Heath

Chapter 7: Mobilization

Introduction: Why Mobilization Is Key

In the grand tapestry of public speaking, mobilization stands as a pivotal thread, connecting the intention of the speaker with the active engagement of the audience. Mobilization is more than just words; it's about motivating, persuading, and rallying individuals to take meaningful actions. It's the moment when a speaker's message transforms into a call to arms, spurring listeners to become doers. Understanding how to effectively mobilize your audience is a skill that can elevate your speeches from mere words to catalysts for change.

Adaptation & Flexibility: Mobilizing Diverse Audience Types

Mobilization is not a one-size-fits-all endeavor. To truly resonate with your audience, you must be adept at adapting your approach based on the diverse characteristics and preferences of those you seek to inspire. Consider Winston Churchill's legendary speeches during World War II. His ability to unite an entire nation under the banner of resolve showcased his knack for mobilizing diverse audience types. Whether addressing the soldiers on the front lines or rallying the civilians at home, Churchill tailored his messages to evoke the specific emotions and motivations needed to propel his audience into action.

Anecdotes: Historical and Recent Examples of Mobilization

Throughout history, mobilization has been a driving force behind monumental shifts. Take, for instance, Martin Luther King Jr.'s "I Have a Dream" speech. His eloquent call for racial equality didn't just outline a vision; it galvanized a movement. More recently, Greta Thunberg's impassioned speeches on climate change have mobilized a global youth movement demanding environmental accountability. These examples underscore the potency of mobilization in shaping the course of events.

Storytelling & Narrative Structure: Inspiring Action

At the heart of effective mobilization lies the power of storytelling. Narratives transcend mere information; they evoke emotions and create connections. Consider Malala Yousafzai, the young Pakistani activist who survived a Taliban assassination attempt. Her compelling story of bravery and determination not only inspired millions but also mobilized support for girls' education worldwide. Crafting your message within a compelling narrative structure can infuse your speeches with the emotional resonance needed to incite action.

Speaker's Canvas Relation: Mobilization in the Framework

Within the realm of the Speaker's Canvas, mobilization represents the culmination of thoughtful preparation, a compelling message, and a relatable messenger. It's the realization of the canvas's interconnected elements, each contributing to the powerful impact of the speech. Without effective mobilization, even the most well-constructed canvas risks falling flat. Mobilization is the force that breathes life into the entire framework, transforming intentions into tangible outcomes.

Emotional Intelligence & Connection: Building Enthusiasm

Mobilization hinges on the speaker's ability to forge a deep connection with the audience. Emotional intelligence is the cornerstone of this connection, enabling you to understand and resonate with the emotions, values, and aspirations of your listeners. President Barack Obama's speeches often displayed this skill, fostering a sense of unity and shared purpose. By tapping into the emotional undercurrents of your audience, you can cultivate genuine enthusiasm and inspire them to action.

Detailed Discussion: Strategies for Effective Mobilization

1. **Clarity of Purpose**: Your mobilization efforts must have a clear and compelling purpose. Define the actionable outcome you seek and ensure your audience understands it.

2. **Inclusive Language**: Tailor your message to resonate with various segments of your audience. Use inclusive language that makes everyone feel like a stakeholder in the cause.

3. **Visual Aids**: Utilize visual aids to amplify your message. Visual representations can reinforce the urgency and importance of the action you're advocating.

4. **Call to Action**: Craft a powerful and concise call to action that leaves no room for ambiguity. Make it easy for your audience to take the desired step.

Rhetorical Techniques: Persuasive Calls to Action

Rhetorical techniques serve as the arsenal of a mobilizing speaker. Employing techniques such as repetition, alliteration, and parallelism can create a memorable and impactful call to action. Consider John F. Kennedy's iconic "Ask not what your country can do for you; ask what you can do for your country." This rhetorical flourish ignited a sense of duty and service in the hearts of Americans, mobilizing them to contribute to their nation's progress.

Practical Advice: Tailoring Mobilization Efforts

1. **Know Your Audience**: Understand the values, concerns, and aspirations of your audience to tailor your message effectively.

2. **Leverage Emotions**: Appeal to emotions that resonate with your cause. Emotionally charged appeals can drive people to take action.

3. **Highlight Urgency**: Clearly communicate the urgency of the issue and why immediate action is essential.

4. **Provide Clear Steps**: Break down the call to action into clear, achievable steps. People are more likely to act when the path forward is evident.

Conclusion: Reflection and Evaluation

In the grand symphony of public speaking, mobilization is the crescendo that leaves a lasting impact. As you reflect on the journey through the seven Ms of the Speaker's Canvas, recognize mobilization as the transformative moment when your words cease to be just words and become catalysts for change. Remember that the effectiveness of your mobilization efforts lies not only in the strength of your message but in your ability to foster genuine connections and inspire action.

Feedback on Mobilization

As you continue to refine your speaking skills, seek feedback on your mobilization efforts. Encourage your listeners to share their thoughts on how your message inspired them to take action. Constructive feedback can help you fine-tune your approach and amplify your mobilization impact.

Introduction: Why Mobilization Is Key

In the grand tapestry of public speaking, mobilization stands as a pivotal thread, connecting the intention of the speaker with the active engagement of the audience. Mobilization is more than just words; it's about motivating, persuading, and rallying individuals to take meaningful actions. It's the moment when a speaker's message transforms into a call to arms, spurring listeners to become doers. Understanding how to effectively mobilize your audience is a skill that can elevate your speeches from mere words to catalysts for change.

Adaptation & Flexibility: Mobilizing Diverse Audience Types

Mobilization is not a one-size-fits-all endeavor. To truly resonate with your audience, you must be adept at adapting your approach based on the diverse characteristics and preferences of those you seek to inspire. Consider Winston Churchill's legendary speeches during World War II. His ability to unite an entire nation under the banner of resolve showcased his knack for mobilizing diverse audience types. Whether addressing the soldiers on the front lines or rallying the civilians at home, Churchill tailored his messages to evoke the specific emotions and motivations needed to propel his audience into action.

Anecdotes: Historical and Recent Examples of Mobilization

Throughout history, mobilization has been a driving force behind monumental shifts. Take, for instance, Martin Luther King Jr.'s "I Have a Dream" speech. His eloquent call for racial equality didn't just outline a vision; it galvanized a movement. More recently, Greta Thunberg's impassioned speeches on climate change have mobilized a global youth movement demanding environmental accountability. These examples underscore the potency of mobilization in shaping the course of events.

Storytelling & Narrative Structure: Inspiring Action

At the heart of effective mobilization lies the power of storytelling. Narratives transcend mere information; they evoke emotions and create connections. Consider Malala Yousafzai, the young Pakistani activist who survived a Taliban assassination attempt. Her compelling story of bravery and determination not only inspired millions but also mobilized support for girls' education worldwide. Crafting your message within a compelling narrative structure can infuse your speeches with the emotional resonance needed to incite action.

Speaker's Canvas Relation: Mobilization in the Framework

Within the realm of the Speaker's Canvas, mobilization represents the culmination of thoughtful preparation, a compelling message, and a relatable messenger. It's the realization of the canvas's interconnected elements, each contributing to the powerful impact of the speech. Without effective mobilization, even the most well-constructed canvas risks falling flat. Mobilization is the force that breathes life into the entire framework, transforming intentions into tangible outcomes.

Emotional Intelligence & Connection: Building Enthusiasm

Mobilization hinges on the speaker's ability to forge a deep connection with the audience. Emotional intelligence is the cornerstone of this connection, enabling you to understand and resonate with the emotions, values, and aspirations of your listeners. President Barack Obama's speeches often displayed this skill, fostering a sense of unity and shared purpose. By tapping into the emotional undercurrents of your audience, you can cultivate genuine enthusiasm and inspire them to action.

Detailed Discussion: Strategies for Effective Mobilization

1. **Clarity of Purpose**: Your mobilization efforts must have a clear and compelling purpose. Define the actionable outcome you seek and ensure your audience understands it.

2. **Inclusive Language**: Tailor your message to resonate with various segments of your audience. Use inclusive language that makes everyone feel like a stakeholder in the cause.

3. **Visual Aids**: Utilize visual aids to amplify your message. Visual representations can reinforce the urgency and importance of the action you're advocating.

4. **Call to Action**: Craft a powerful and concise call to action that leaves no room for ambiguity. Make it easy for your audience to take the desired step.

Rhetorical Techniques: Persuasive Calls to Action

Rhetorical techniques serve as the arsenal of a mobilizing speaker. Employing techniques such as repetition, alliteration, and parallelism can create a memorable and impactful call to action. Consider John F. Kennedy's iconic "Ask not what your country can do for you; ask what you can do for your country." This rhetorical flourish ignited a sense of duty and service in the hearts of Americans, mobilizing them to contribute to their nation's progress.

Practical Advice: Tailoring Mobilization Efforts

1. **Know Your Audience**: Understand the values, concerns, and aspirations of your audience to tailor your message effectively.

2. **Leverage Emotions**: Appeal to emotions that resonate with your cause. Emotionally charged appeals can drive people to take action.

3. **Highlight Urgency**: Clearly communicate the urgency of the issue and why immediate action is essential.

4. **Provide Clear Steps**: Break down the call to action into clear, achievable steps. People are more likely to act when the path forward is evident.

Conclusion: Reflection and Evaluation

In the grand symphony of public speaking, mobilization is the crescendo that leaves a lasting impact. As you reflect on the journey through the seven Ms of the Speaker's Canvas, recognize mobilization as the transformative moment when your words cease to be just words and become catalysts for change. Remember that the effectiveness of your mobilization efforts lies not only in the strength of your message but in your ability to foster genuine connections and inspire action.

Feedback on Mobilization

As you continue to refine your speaking skills, seek feedback on your mobilization efforts. Encourage your listeners to share their thoughts on how your message inspired them to take action. Constructive feedback can help you fine-tune your approach and amplify your mobilization impact.

Conclusion: Your Voice Matters

Preparation

Preparation is not merely a step; it's the bedrock of any speech. It's where the process of understanding the 7 Ms begins. Research, planning, and foresight lay the foundation for success, cutting across all other elements.

Messenger

The speaker – You – are the human connection that brings words to life. Authenticity, credibility, and understanding of oneself play a pivotal role in connecting with the audience.

Message

The essence of what you want to say; your message is the core around which everything else revolves. It's your vision, your argument, your call to action. It must be clear, compelling, and focused.

Medium

The channels through which your message will travel to reach the audience. Understanding the medium's nuances allows you to tailor your delivery for optimal impact, whether live or recorded, spoken, or written.

Monitoring

Speechmaking doesn't end with applause; it's about understanding the lasting impact, observing shifts in sentiment, and tangible changes. Monitoring is the feedback loop that fuels growth and adaptation.

Mobilization

Your speech can move people to think, feel, and act. Mobilization is about making that connection tangible, aligning your call-to-action with your audience's needs, and creating a momentum that lasts.

Members

Your audience is not a faceless mass; they are individuals with unique perspectives, needs, and desires. Understanding them enables you to create a speech that resonates on a personal and emotional level.

Moment

Every speech is an opportunity, a moment in time that you and your audience share. Recognizing the uniqueness of each moment adds depth and significance to your words.

The Speechmaking Journey

A speech is not just a performance; it's a project, an undertaking that requires planning, execution, monitoring, and reflection. It's a craft that demands continuous learning, experimentation, and empathy.

Moreover, speechmaking is not confined to stages, auditoriums, or political arenas. It's an everyday activity, a tool to express ideas, connect with others, persuade, inform, and inspire. Whether you're speaking at a friend's funeral, giving a valedictory address, leading a business meeting, or engaging in a casual conversation, the principles of the 7 Ms apply.

Your voice is not merely an instrument; it's a gift. The world needs to hear your unique perspective, your ideas, your stories. The 7 Ms Canvas serves as a guide, a tool to help you navigate the intricate art of speaking.

Remember, the words you speak can create a ripple effect, impacting lives, shaping opinions, and changing the world, one speech at a time.

Embrace the journey of speechmaking, for it's never a one-time event. It's a lifelong pursuit, an opportunity to make a difference. Your voice matters. Let it be heard.

Recommended Reading

- "The Art of Public Speaking" by Dale Carnegie
- "Speak Like Churchill, Stand Like Lincoln" by James C. Humes
- "TED Talks: The Official TED Guide to Public Speaking" by Chris Anderson

Appendix: The Speaker's Canvas & The 7Ms

The 7 Ms Speaker's Canvas is a visual and conceptual tool designed to facilitate the understanding and execution of an effective speech. It organizes the essential components of public speaking into a cohesive and interconnected framework.

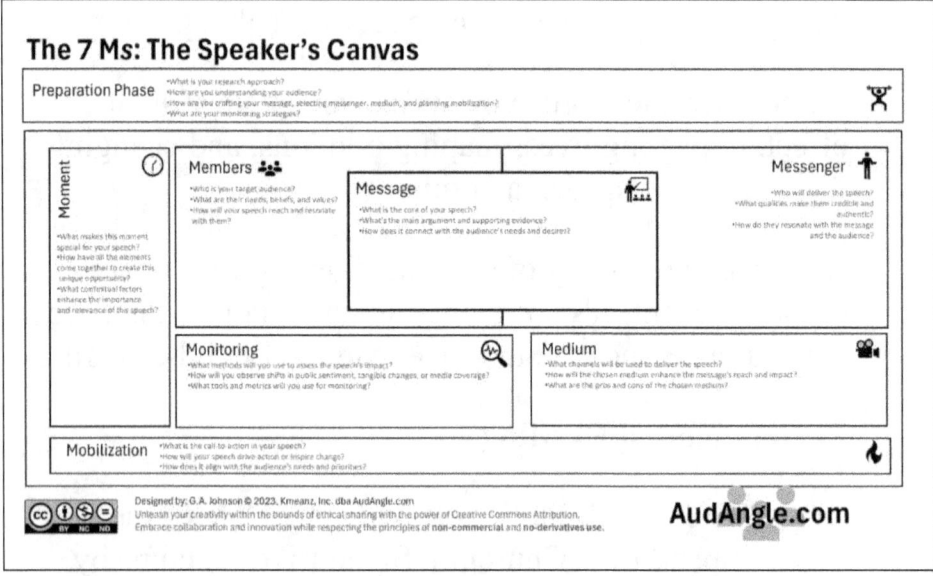

1. Centricity of the Message

- **Importance**: At the core of the canvas is the Message. It's where the convergence of the Messenger and the Members happens, representing the essence of the speech.
- **Implications**: The Message is what binds everything together. It's the main argument, the vision, the purpose, and it informs and influences every other element on the canvas.

2. Proximity of Elements

- **Messenger & Members**: Positioned on either side of the Message, these elements reflect the human connection. The Messenger is the voice, while the Members are the ears. Together, they complete the communication cycle.
- **Monitoring & Mobilization**: Located at the foundation, these elements represent the response and action. Mobilization drives the call-to-action, while Monitoring assesses the impact, allowing for continuous refinement.

3. Interconnectedness of the Ms

- **Preparation**: Encapsulates the planning and research, setting the stage for all other elements.
- **Medium**: Acts as the conduit for the Message, connecting the Messenger with the Members.
- **Moment**: The culmination, where all elements come together, creating a unique and special instance in time.

4. The Canvas as a Tool

- **Practical Application**: The canvas can be used by anyone, from students to professionals, to craft and deliver effective speeches.
- **Strategic Alignment**: By visualizing the components, the canvas ensures that each element aligns and contributes to the overall goal of the speech.

Conclusion

The Speaker's Canvas is more than a diagram; it's a philosophy, a way to understand and approach speechmaking. The centrality of the Message signifies the meeting of minds, the point where understanding, persuasion, and inspiration take place.

Mobilization forms the foundation, translating words into action, while Monitoring ensures that the speech's impact is understood, measured, and refined.

By highlighting the proximity and relationship between these elements, the canvas becomes a versatile tool, guiding speakers in crafting speeches that resonate, influence, and endure.

Whether you are an aspiring speaker or an experienced orator, the Speaker's Canvas provides a roadmap, helping you navigate the complex yet rewarding journey of public speaking. It's where your voice finds its purpose and your words find their mark.

www.ingramcontent.com/pod-product-compliance
Lightning Source LLC
Chambersburg PA
CBHW050537300426
44113CB00012B/2146